To my special dad, Alexander McKie (1922–2012), who fought so bravely and succumbed to end-stage motor neurone disease while I was writing this book during the historic summer of 2012.

Alice Muir is a Chartered Psychologist and qualified teacher of psychology, and also an experienced trainer, university lecturer, community group worker, stress adviser and life coach. Through these roles, she has supported hundreds of people with depression, and since 1994 has trained stress advisers in the UK and overseas.

Alice is a member of the General Teaching Council and the Association for Coaching, a chartered member of the British Psychological Society and a Fellow of the International Stress Management Association (ISMA UK). She is currently the features editor of the ISMA's quarterly journal *Stress News* and also writes a column in the journal. She has written a range of blended learning self-development courses and packs, as well as self-help books on depression, stress, NLP and relaxation.

Alice is married with two grown-up children. As a young woman, she experienced bouts of depression, both before having her children and while they were small.

Overcoming Depression

Alice Muir

Also available
in ebook

Contents

Introduction

When I sat down to write this book, I began it in the same way as my previous nine books; I did the research, thought around the subject and reflected on what I believed someone who was depressed or who wanted to know about depression would want to read. I've been writing, coaching and running workshops on depression for several decades, and have added to my background knowledge and experience with books on post-natal depression, stress, anxiety and loneliness.

Then I began the actual writing: Introduction; Chapter 1; paragraph 1. A first paragraph was written, then another and another. Introduction written. Great, well under way. But as I progressed through Chapter 1, instead of the writing becoming easier as usual, the work began to slow down and become very heavy-going, and my mind began to drift. This had never happened before. What was the problem?

I looked back at the Introduction I had already written and pressed the delete button. Then I began writing this Introduction. Why? The problem was that I had depression myself when I was 18; this lasted for some time, and it was a very difficult time in my life. And I couldn't write this book without mentioning this and building my experiences and personal insight into what I was writing. I felt I owed it to readers who have depression to be honest with them. So this is a new introduction, a new start for me and the book. And the book I finished in October 2012 is very different from the one I started to write in May 2012.

When I wrote the Introduction, it was the spring of 2012 and there was an exciting summer ahead, with the Queen's Diamond Jubilee celebrations and the London Olympics, and, on a more personal note, my second grandchild due to be born in late July. However, just after I began writing, my father went into hospital, where he was diagnosed with end-stage motor neurone disease (MND) and given only months to live. This book has been a supportive companion, providing me with a refuge over the summer while the father I knew and loved disappeared more and more quickly into the prison created by a body that would do less and less for him, leaving him finally unable to speak, open his eyes or make himself understood, although his mind was not affected. Dad died peacefully at midnight on 6 September 2012. At the other end of life's unpredictable journey, my beautiful granddaughter bounced into the world safely on 18 July, perfect in every way and with piercing blue eyes. The summer of 2012, and writing this book, is something I'll never forget.

Alice Muir
Chartered Psychologist/Writer

October 2012

Part 1:
Information

1

Understanding depression

It is common to hear the word 'depressed' used in throwaway comments like 'I'm feeling really depressed about my job', or 'This weather is so depressing'. Maybe people who talk like that are clinically depressed, but it's much more likely that they are simply a bit 'fed-up', or 'down in the dumps', something which happens to us all from time to time. Everyone feels low, blue or unhappy sometimes.

But if feelings like these are interfering with your life and go on all day, and for more than a couple of weeks, or if they keep coming back for a few days at a time, it could be a sign that you are medically depressed, in which case you should be doing something about it.

How do you feel?

1 Are you feeling any of these right now? (Choose as many as apply.)

    a   Fed-up
    b   In low spirits
    c   Down
    d   Depressed
    e   None of these

2 Have you felt any of these in the past few weeks? (Choose as many as apply.)

    a   Tearful
    b   No energy
    c   Over-reacting to everything
    d   That no-one understands
    e   None of these

3 Do you feel you know what depression is? (Choose as many as apply.)

    a   Not sure
    b   Yes
    c   No
    d   Have a rough idea

4 If you have experience of depression yourself or in another person, how long did this last?

    a   Less than a month
    b   A few months
    c   About six months
    d   More than six months

5 Which of these people has had depression? (Choose as many as apply.)

    a   Robbie Williams (singer with Take That)
    b   Sir Winston Churchill (British prime minister during World War II)
    c   Gwyneth Paltrow (actress)
    d   David Walliams (actor and comedian from *Little Britain*)
    e   None of them.

Why read this book?

This is a book for anyone who wants to know more about depression and how to cope better with it, maybe for themselves or maybe for someone else. It's user friendly, informed and informative, and written by someone who knows what depression feels like.

Depression can affect anyone, both men and women, from any background and at any age. The answer to Question 5 above is 'all of them'. Even the rich and famous get depressed. As I was writing this book, I was surprised at how many celebrities revealed for the first time that they had been depressed. One of these was David Walliams, who disclosed in October 2012 that he'd had depression, and that he had gone into rehab at the start of his career to deal with depression following the break up of a relationship.

Most people either have personal experience of depression, as I do, or know someone close to them who has. I have several friends and relatives who have been depressed. Perhaps you do too. Several people in your street, or nearby, will be experiencing its effects right now. Appendix 1 has more information and guidance for those who have a friend or loved one with depression and want to know how best to help them. Children can become depressed too, and Appendix 3 has more information about this.

It can be very difficult to know what to do if you're depressed. How can you find help? You may not know what's wrong, or the questions to ask or who to ask for help. You just know that something is very wrong without knowing what, and that's a really scary way to feel. Who can you trust enough to talk about it? What will they think of you? And what about your job? Coping at work can grow harder and harder, but as long as you can keep going and do your job, you hope no-one will notice you're a bit down.

Being depressed is not only distressing, but it can feel painful inside. It is disabling, and it saps your energy and enthusiasm for life as well as your energy and motivation to do something about the way you are feeling. If you trip and break your wrist, it will also be distressing, disabling and painful, but it won't take away your energy and zest for life or your energy for seeking help. You just dial 999, and the emergency services will arrive and sort you out. If only it were that easy when you're depressed. This book will try to improve that situation for you, and show you the way forward, and how to build up the energy to take action.

Mythbuster

Myth: People who are depressed could 'pull themselves together' and 'snap out of it' if they tried hard enough.

Truth: No, they couldn't! No more than you can 'snap out of' the flu or a broken arm.

What is depression?

What is depression? What brings it on? What can you do about it? There are so many questions, often with a fear of the unknown. This book will explain what depression is, how it can make you feel, and what you can do about it. Reading a book like this will not provide an immediate solution, but it will answer these questions and others you didn't know you had, as well as giving you straightforward ways to cope better and feel more in control. You won't find any heavy medical explanations, although if you are interested in these, Appendix 4 gives details of where to find such information. Your doctor is also a good first contact.

> 'It was as if I was cut-off from everything around me. My feelings had sort of gone flat. It's hard to explain. Fun, love, everyday life – all seemed muffled, as if they were behind a screen, and I couldn't get to them.'

> Jade

You'll find ideas and information to think about throughout the book, as well as checklists and questionnaires to use if you wish to. But I know that depression can make everything seem an effort, so you can always come back to these on a better day if you need to. It does help to have to hand a small notebook and pen or, if you prefer, a loose-leaf folder, a netbook or laptop. That way, you can jot down answers to questionnaires or make a note of anything you've found particularly helpful. But be sure to keep these notes safe; they are just for your eyes. Alternatively, you might find it easier to make an audio recording, or to make notes on your mobile phone.

At the beginning of each chapter there will be a short assessment like the one you've just completed, to give you the chance to rate yourself on how you feel, and to get you thinking about some of the key issues to be discussed in that chapter.

Point to remember

You'll find everything in this book friendly, straightforward and easy to follow, with as little jargon as possible. Move through the chapters at your own pace, or dip in and out of the book to suit your interests. Don't worry if you find you have to reread some pages. Depression tends to make concentrating difficult. Give yourself whatever time you need, and don't overdo it. You can use this book as a reference later too. I'm sorry to say I can't provide any overnight miracle cures – I wish I could – but what you'll read will help you to understand depression better, and get you started on the path to recovery.

How common is depression?

Mental health problems are more common than you might expect. At any one time in the UK, 300 out of 1,000 people will be experiencing a mental health problem of some kind. That's three people in every ten. So in your city, town or village right now, three in every ten people do not feel well psychologically.

The Kings Fund reported in 2007, that 1.25 million people in England were depressed. In 2012, the Royal College of Psychiatrists estimated that one person in five will experience depression of some kind at some point in their lives. With so many people suffering in this way, it's surprising we don't hear more about it. One reason is that many people don't tell even close friends and relatives they are depressed, because there is still a stigma surrounding mental health. According to the NHS (2012), depression is the fourth most common cause of disability and disease worldwide, and the World Health Organization has said (2012) that depression will be the most common cause of ill health in the developed world by 2020. We don't live in a very happy world.

The NHS describes depression as the most common mental health disorder in the UK, and the most common reason for consulting a doctor. Every year in the UK, 6 per cent of adults will experience a period of depression, and more than 15 per cent (or around one in six) will experience depression during their lifetime.

So when you are in the doctor's waiting room, the majority of other patients are likely to be there because they are depressed.

Women are more likely than men to have an episode of depression which needs treatment.

According to the NHS (2012), one in four women and one in ten men in the UK will experience depression that needs treatment at some point during their lifetime.

Point to remember

Healthcare professionals use different terms for what the general public would call 'depression'. These terms include 'major depressive disorder', 'clinical depression' and 'medical depression'. 'Dysthymia' is an expression that is sometimes used when a person has had a few mild symptoms, but these have lasted for two years or more. For simplicity, I'll just use 'depression' to mean any of these. Other types of depression will be explained in Chapter 2.

Recognizing depression

Depression isn't about feeling 'fed-up' now and then, or upset by some bad news, unless the feelings continue over weeks or months. Have a look through these signs of depression.

If for the past month, you have experienced three or four of the following on more days than not, you may be depressed and should see your doctor.

► Waking up early, having difficulty sleeping, or sleeping more than usual

► Finding it hard to concentrate or make decisions

► Crying a lot for no clear reason

► Socializing much less than normal

► Feeling tired with no energy, and as if everything is an effort

► Physical aches and pains with no physical cause

► Feeling low-spirited for much of the time, more days than not

► Getting no pleasure out of anything

► Losing interest in your sex life

► Blaming yourself and feeling guilty when you wouldn't usually

► Lacking self-confidence and self-esteem

► Having many negative thoughts

► Not eating properly, and losing or putting on weight

► Feeling helpless or empty

► Self-harming (e.g. cutting yourself, overdosing, burning yourself with cigarettes)

► Distancing yourself from others; not asking for support

► Being unusually pessimistic about the future

► Thinking about death or suicide most days.

If your score is borderline or, despite your score, you're still not sure whether you have depression, it's advisable to see your doctor for an assessment. It doesn't always show itself in clear ways, especially if it's mild.

Like other illnesses, depression can be mild, moderate or severe. Here is how you can recognize the difference.

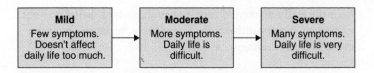

Mild	**Moderate**	**Severe**
Few symptoms. Doesn't affect daily life too much.	More symptoms. Daily life is difficult.	Many symptoms. Daily life is very difficult.

Even if depression seems mild, it doesn't mean you shouldn't see the doctor. Mild depression, left untreated for weeks or months, can still make life more colourless than it should be and can easily develop into something more serious.

Many people find that they are both anxious and depressed at the same time. These feelings are not opposites. You can feel down about a promotion that didn't work out, but also be worried about what that means for your future plans. It's a very common everyday mix of feelings.

If you are having suicidal thoughts, or find yourself planning how you could take your own life, you should see your doctor or another health professional immediately. You'll find more on suicidal behaviour in Appendix 2, and contact details for organizations offering information and support in Appendix 4.

Case study: Amy

Amy, aged 29, had sailed through school and university, and straight into a job in graphic design. Life was good. She'd been working for five years and was saving up to buy a flat when, out of the blue, she was made redundant. She tried to get another job, but had no luck, and within a few months, she had to move back in with her parents. Although she got on well with her parents, it felt bad having to go back home. Gradually, over the following months, she would sleep in later and later in the morning, then watch daytime TV. Soon, she couldn't be bothered getting dressed to go out with her friends. Amy thought she was just fed up at losing her job, but she was actually becoming depressed.

SELF-HARM

Harming yourself by cutting your arms, banging your head, scratching or burning your skin, binge drinking etc can be part of depression, although it can also indicate that someone is emotionally distressed rather than depressed. Self-harm can give a release or outlet to emotional pain, or be the outcome of very low self-esteem or self-hatred, but it isn't usually a suicide attempt.

Diana, Princess of Wales, was a self-harmer during her marriage to the Prince of Wales, and celebrities such as the actor Russell Brand and athlete Dame Kelly Holmes have talked about their experiences of injuring themselves. There is more information about self-harm in Appendix 2, with contact details of support organizations in Appendix 4.

Myths about depression

1 Depression is a sign of weakness

Depression can happen to both weak and strong personalities. It's mostly brought on by circumstances or physical changes we have no control over. Some of the world's strongest and most successful people have been depressed. These include Abraham Lincoln, Winston Churchill and, more recently, Jack Straw, a former Home Secretary, and Alasdair Campbell, former 'spin doctor' to Tony Blair.

2 Attempting suicide is just attention-seeking, and shouldn't be taken as a serious risk to life

All suicide attempts should be taken seriously.

3 People who self-harm are manipulative and attention-seeking

After a major study, the organization SANE found that the opposite was true. Self-harming is usually a hidden form of behaviour. It is a coping strategy, and mainly about hiding feelings and thoughts. SANE found that the majority of those who self-harm actively try to conceal it from their family.

The effects of depression

Your whole mind and body are affected when you're depressed. It has an impact on almost everything you do, though sometimes you aren't aware of it and only realize later, when you're feeling more like yourself. Here are some of those effects. Read through them. Can you identify with any of these?

Your body and behaviour	How you think and feel
Weepy	Sad and alone
Spending much more time than usual in bed or on the sofa	Don't feel like doing anything
	Useless
Slow	A failure
Sleep disturbed during the night	Can't be bothered with anything
Early morning wakening	Worried
Hard to concentrate	Bored
Weary	Depressed
Everything's an effort	Thoughts about death and suicide
Tired all the time	Stressed
Taking daytime naps	Nothing gives pleasure any more
Tense	Fed-up and low
Sleeping more/sleeping less	Anxious
Eating more/eating less	Feel you can't cope with things
Weight gain/weight loss	No point in anything
Self-harming	Go over and over things in your mind
Avoiding other people	Panicky
Memory not good	No-one likes me
Don't do things you used to enjoy	No-one cares

Quick fix

Rather than using the label 'depressed', try thinking of 'being down' or 'having a low mood'. It's the same thing, but it somehow feels easier to deal with and less of a heavy burden to carry.

Recovery and recurrence

It's difficult to say how soon you will feel better; that depends on how severe your depression is, how long you've felt depressed, and whether or not you have had treatment of some kind. Untreated, the average length of an episode of depression is six to eight months, though some people can experience symptoms for much longer.

You are likely to feel an improvement within two to three weeks of beginning any treatment and should then continue to improve, although possibly in a stop–start fashion, until you're feeling like your old self again. So it may take several months to reach full recovery, and longer if you've been severely depressed.

It is possible that you will feel depressed again. Around half of those who have had one episode of depression will have another at some point in their life. If you've had several bouts, it is more likely you may have another. I had one major bout of depression and then several minor brushes with it. Through experience, I got to know the triggers that could make me feel down again, and I learned to recognize the slight changes in my thinking or behaviour that usually indicated something was beginning to change. So I was able to take action early, and avoid going into a full-blown downer.

Triggers are personal to each of us, and can be almost anything. Here are some typical triggers.

▶ A major life change, or more than one at the same time

▶ Stress

▶ Ending an important relationship, or a problem relationship

▶ Ending treatment too soon

▶ Being criticized or bullied

▶ Long, dark winter months

▶ A major disappointment

▶ Loneliness

▶ Hormonal changes

▶ Inactivity

▶ A failure of some kind

▶ Physical illness in yourself or a loved one

▶ Boredom

▶ Sleep deprivation or exhaustion

▶ A loss of any kind.

Your thinking space

What do you think your triggers might be? Think back to the months before you were feeling down.

❋ What was going on in your life?

❋ How were you feeling?

If it's all a bit of a blank, or there is nothing you can put your finger on, think about it over the next few weeks, and maybe ask those who know you well what they remember. Sometimes those around us see things that we don't.

Apart from looking out for triggers and early signs, it helps not to be in denial about your depression and the chance of relapse. If you think about it, it's no different from a physical condition such as eczema, or watching your weight. It makes sense to think about prevention. Being able to handle stress better and building up your resilience to depression also help to prevent a relapse (see Chapter 11). Mindfulness has also been shown to provide some protection against a setback (Chapter 7).

Quick fix

If you are depressed, baby steps will get you there. So take one day at a time, or one hour at a time if a day's too long.

Next steps

The key points covered in Chapter 2 are:

❋ **different types of depression**

❋ **why do people get depressed?**

❋ **can you bring it on yourself?**

❋ **how loss and bereavement can affect you**

❋ **stress, anxiety and depression.**

2

Types of depression and its causes

Depression isn't just one standard illness, the same for everyone who experiences it. Unlike toothache or a cold, which affect everyone in much the same way, everyone's experience of depression will be different. Like rain, it can present itself in different ways, at different times and for many different reasons: a light shower, a constant drizzle, an unexpected downpour, a thunderstorm or part of a bigger pattern of sunshine and showers. Depression and low mood can also appear at important points in our lives, or certain times of year. It can be mild and pass quickly, or be more severe and last much longer. This chapter will explain this variety, and what commonly used terms mean.

How do you feel?

1 Do you feel anxious now, or have you been anxious recently?

   a Yes
   b No
   c Not sure

2 Do you feel well a lot of the time, but can often feel a bit down?

   a Yes
   b No
   c Not sure

3 If you are a mother, did you feel a bit tearful and down for a short time a few days after giving birth?

   a Yes
   b No

4 Did you feel down or depressed for many weeks or months in the year or so after giving birth?

   a Yes
   b No

5 Are there times when you feel exceptionally happy, elated and full of energy and ideas - and this alternates with times when you feel very tired, down and depressed?

   a Yes
   b No
   c Not sure

6 Have other members of your family experienced any of these? (tick any that apply):

   a Depression of any kind
   b Obsessive-compulsive disorder (OCD)
   c Panic attacks
   d Anxiety
   e Difficulty coping with stress.

The different names for depression

Chapter 1 mentioned how various healthcare professionals use different terms for what many simply call 'depression'.

Professionals use terms like 'major depressive disorder', 'clinical depression' or 'medical depression'. This is because depression can appear in a range of guises, producing different symptoms, and healthcare workers have two very detailed classification systems available to help them to identify which they are dealing with. One is produced by the American Psychiatric Association (APA) and the other by the World Health Organization (WHO). This means that many different terms are used to describe the type and severity of depression. Sometimes the same condition may be given different names.

Point to remember

Both the APA and WHO see depression, whatever its exact type, as a disorder of our 'mood'. On first hearing, this sounds odd. But if you think about heart disorders, skin disorders or eye disorders, it becomes more understandable. Just as your heart, skin or eyes may not be operating properly, there can be something not working properly about your mood, about how you feel within yourself. This important process is not functioning the way it should. So health professionals call depression a 'mood disorder'.

We don't need to concern ourselves with the full range and criteria for the various names and labels attached to depression (although details are given in Appendix 4 for anyone who wants to know more). All you really need to know is that:

▶ depression is brought about when our mood regulation system is faulty

▶ health professionals often use the word 'affect' in place of the word 'mood'

▶ the terms 'medical depression' or 'clinical depression' are used so that we can distinguish between occasionally feeling fed-up or blue and a persistent condition that is interfering with everyday life

▶ the term 'dysthymia' is used for a milder form of depression that has come and gone for over two years or more

▶ the terms 'mild', 'moderate' and 'severe' and 'major' or 'minor' are often used to indicate how serious the depression is (see Chapter 1).

Quick fix

Whenever you get the chance, hug someone you love or your pet, or squeeze a big lovable cuddly toy.

Different types of depression

You'll probably be aware that there isn't just one kind of depression that we've talked about so far. There are other forms of depression that are sufficiently different which I shall now explain, so that you'll have a basic understanding of these too. Many films, books and storylines in serial dramas like soap operas feature these other illnesses.

POST-NATAL DEPRESSION (PND)

Many mothers have 'the baby blues' around three to five days after the birth of their baby, when they feel weepy and down. This usually passes by the tenth day after the birth without any treatment. Post-natal depression is a more serious problem, affecting one in ten new mothers. It can appear from two weeks to a few months or more after the birth. Current research suggests this depression is not hormonal, but more to do with tiredness, lack of sleep and the massive changes in lifestyle that a new baby brings, especially for older parents who have waited to start a family until they have already established a comfortable way of life. New fathers can also be affected.

A very few women, 1 in 1,000, will develop a rare and serious illness called post-natal psychosis (PNP) after giving birth. The 'psychosis' aspect of this condition means that they may see things that are not there and develop strange beliefs and ideas. They may not be aware of this, as the illness makes it difficult for someone to be aware that they're behaving unusually. PNP must be treated in hospital, and there are specialist units which take the mother and her baby.

BIPOLAR DISORDER

With this illness (previously called manic depression), periods of depression alternate with periods of 'mania'. This can form a regular pattern, although this is not always the case. 'Bipolar' means there are two 'poles' or extremes, and your mood swings back and forth between them. This change in mood can happen gradually over weeks or months, or it can be rapid and frequent. When manic, the sufferer is in a state of high excitement, and may form grand plans and fantastic schemes and try to put them into action, usually with distressing outcomes.

But outcomes are not always negative. It's not uncommon for people with this disorder to be highly creative in their manic phase, only to pay for this later with a period of deep depression. There are many well-known examples, both today and from history. Florence Nightingale and Vincent van Gogh are believed to have been bipolar, as was the actress Vivien Leigh and the writer Virginia Woolf. The singers Ray Davies, Sinead O'Connor and Kerry Katona, actress Linda Hamilton, comedian Ruby Wax and broadcaster Steven Fry have all been diagnosed with bipolar disorder. This condition is treatable, usually with medication, the most commonly prescribed being Lithium.

SEASONAL AFFECTIVE DISORDER (SAD)

If your depression has an annual pattern and appears only in the autumn and winter, it could be caused by not getting enough daylight. Estimates vary, but seasonal affective disorder (SAD) affects around seven in every hundred of the population in the UK, and is most likely to occur in December, January and February. It's more common in the more northern lattitudes of the nothern hemisphere (and more southern latitudes in the southern hemisphere).

Sunlight and bright daylight trigger the production of serotonin in the brain. Serotonin is a key component in the brain chemistry which keeps moods stable, realistic and positive. So you may benefit from spending more time outside on bright days, or sitting in front of a special light box designed to treat the disorder (see Appendix 4 for details). This condition often responds to similar treatments to depression, including antidepressant medication.

Mythbuster

Myth: Some people are depressed just to get attention.

Truth: Nonsense! There are so many better ways you could get attention. And besides, you can't **make** yourself depressed.

Depression's companions

For some people, depression and low mood are their main problems, with no other difficulties or symptoms. But more often you can find you have other problems too. Most commonly, you may feel anxious or stressed. The Mental Health Foundation reported in 2012 that the most common mental health problem in the UK is to have anxiety and depression together, called 'mixed anxiety and depression'. It's also not unusual when you're depressed to have panic attacks or develop phobic behaviour, e.g. avoiding situations such as socializing, queuing or shopping. Mild obsessive or compulsive behaviours are also common. I certainly experienced the latter, checking several times that I had switched off the gas ring before leaving the house, but still remaining anxious that I hadn't done it. Worrying thoughts would pop into my head, and wouldn't go away: 'This headache is so bad, it must be a brain tumour'. In a minority of these cases, this can develop into obsessive-compulsive disorder (OCD).

To the person experiencing all this, it's not always clear which came first – the stress, anxiety, OCD or the depression – or whether they appeared at the same time. It used to be thought that anxiety, stress, OCD and depression were all separate and unrelated, but it's now clear that if stress doesn't resolve itself fairly quickly but goes on for weeks or months, it can lead to any of these conditions. Examples of this kind of unending stress are if you're being bullied at work or have serious debts with no possibility of paying them off.

On the other hand, being depressed makes carrying on with everyday life and your work extremely difficult, and that can itself create stress with no end in sight. So, as I've said already, sometimes it's not easy to work out which came first, the stress or the depression. And just to complicate matters, depression can appear for no apparent reason, although when you look back, you can usually work out what caused it.

Your thinking space

Do you mainly feel depressed, or do you feel anxious sometimes too?

Is there an obvious source of stress in your life right now?

Looking back with hindsight, did the stress begin:

✳ around the same time as the depression?

✳ a few weeks or months before the depression?

✳ after the depression began?

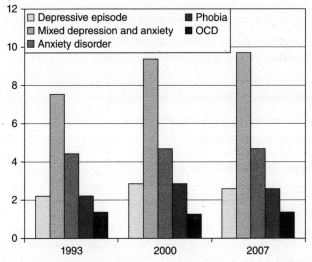

Percentage of people aged 16–64 experiencing depression, anxiety, phobia or OCD (MIND)

On a more positive note, research shows that if you treat the depression, you will treat all of these other conditions too. Chapter 11 will tell you more about stress and panic attacks, and the ways you can make a difference to these. For now, here are some figures from MIND's seven-yearly survey on anxiety, mixed anxiety/depression, and depressive episodes since 2000.

WHY DEPRESSION IS WORSE THAN AN INJURY

If you trip and sprain your ankle, or strain a muscle in a football game with friends, or break an arm on a ski-ing holiday, would any of these be easier to cope with than depression? Or if you have the flu, or have to have your appendix out, or a wisdom tooth extracted? Are these illnesses and health problems easier to get through than depression?

From my own experiences, I reckon all of these physical conditions have at least seven advantages over feeling depressed – would you agree with any of these?

1 People can see what's wrong with you.

2 Everyone understands these common health problems.

3 It's obvious these conditions are real, and not imagined or 'all in your head', as others might think or even say to you.

4 These conditions aren't embarrassing or something to be ashamed of and kept hidden or a secret.

5 You and other people know roughly how long it takes to recover from these conditions.

6 People know what to say to you.

7 People don't avoid you.

Maybe you can add some others.

 Quick fix

Look at a picture which always makes you smile. Keep lots of these by your side or in your pocket or bag, all the time – like a paper hankie, ready for when you sneeze.

Knowing why you're depressed

Knowing why you are depressed won't make the depression go away, but it can help in other ways. My grandson had severe eczema from the age of six weeks, so bad that he had to have ointment applied all over his body three times a day, and had to be bandaged everywhere except his head. The ointment eased the redness and itching and lessened the likelihood of infection, but the treatment was just keeping it at bay; the condition was still as severe. The whole family was affected. My daughter, a first-time mother, felt guilty, convinced she was doing something wrong and that it was her fault. I felt powerless too, unable to help my first grandchild. This went on for almost a year, until the local hospital agreed to do allergy tests. The tests discovered a severe allergy to eggs and nuts, which had been coming through to the baby in his mother's milk. Although he still needs creams and bandages, removing these foods from his diet produced a miraculous improvement in his skin. Can you think of a situation in your life, or that of someone close to you, which improved when the cause was discovered?

Depression can be like that too. Even if you only have a vague idea of the cause, it:

▶ won't feel so much like a bolt from the blue

▶ helps you to know how best to make it better

▶ gives you back some control

▶ helps you to feel less guilty

▶ confirms that it's not your fault.

Mythbuster

Myth: Depression is just the way we all feel if something bad happens.

Truth: Everyone gets disappointed and sad when something bad happens in their life. But that's not the same as depression. And depression can even happen when everything's going well – a fact that sometimes confuses people who are depressed, and makes them feel even more down and guilty than they are already.

A personal journal

I suggest that you begin to keep a simple diary, or personal journal. This won't be a 'daily entry describing what you did today' type of diary. As mentioned in Chapter 1, all you will need is something in which to record your answers to the assessments that start each chapter, and for working on any other activities in the book: a notebook, a beautifully designed journal, a page per day diary, a loose-leaf folder, your mobile phone, i-Pad, laptop or tablet, or you could make an audio-recording – whatever you're most comfortable with.

Making special notes every day can be help in your recovery. Many people have found this easy, helpful and effective. Even if the idea is a turn-off for you, I urge you to give it a chance. It doesn't have to take much time, and it can make a real difference. Studies have shown that doing this regularly can lift your mood significantly.

Saturday	Sunday	Monday
3/10	4/10	5/10
1. Text from Emma	1. Sunny morning	1. Film on TV was good.
2. Found ring I'd lost	2. Mum rang	2. Lazy bath.
3. Pasta wasn't over-cooked	3. Favourite track on radio	3. Tom cooked.

Here are two straightforward things you can include in your journal to get you started.

1 Each day, make a brief note of how you feel. You can use a word or phrase, such as 'sad', 'down', 'more positive today', 'good', 'fair'. Or maybe use an appropriate 'smiley' (or emoticon). Or if numbers appeal more, score your day on 1–10 or 1–100 scale. How you do this is up to you, and is only limited by your energy and imagination. When you look back, it really helps you to see when the good days and bad days were, and perhaps to see reasons for these. And sometimes it can show that you've had more good days than you thought. It's easy when you're depressed only to remember the tough days.

2 Every evening, take a few moments to think over your day, and write down three good or positive things that happened. These don't need to be anything big or special: a text from a friend, something interesting in a magazine, something delicious to eat, a glimmer of sunshine, your dog running

to meet you when you came home. Start by doing this every day, then maybe three or four times a week. At the end of the week, read over all the positive things you've written.

Causes of depression

Until the past few decades, little was known about why people became depressed and the treatments available now – talking therapies and medications – weren't well established. But that has all changed. We now know that depression has a number of possible causes, and treatments have been developed to target these more precisely, making them much more effective. The remainder of the chapter will tell you about some the most common reasons for people becoming depressed, and in so doing, perhaps make it easier to understand your own depression, or that of someone you know.

Your thinking space

Has depression crept up on you? There are many different causes or triggers for depression, and in many cases, depression comes on gradually, meaning that you may not notice what's happening to you.

* Think about how you were six months ago. Remember what you were doing, and what your average day was like. How does that compare with how you feel now? What about a year ago? Two years ago? Or longer?

* Looking back like this can give you a much better perspective on how things have changed, and how you may have changed too. You can sometimes see how your low mood has coincided with some other event.

* Have you put your increasingly depressed feelings down to your situation, and just worked harder and longer to try to sort out the situation? You can become afraid to stop doing working on this, because it would allow you to think, and that just makes you feel worse. Or you're scared you won't want to get back on the merry-go-round again. This can leave you feeling exhausted and burnt-out, with no energy or fight left.

Stop searching everywhere, trying to find the answer to all your worries. If you can stand still sometimes, it will be much easier for the answers to find you.

Research into what causes depression is going on all the time in many different disciplines. There are real physiological changes that explain depression, which puts paid to the idea that we can 'shake ourselves out of it', or 'get a life'.

> 'Today's informed psychiatrists will not be able to deny the role of the brain in the mental ailments that afflict their patients.'
>
> Arango, Underwood and Mann, 2002
> (USA research team)

At the time of writing, seven general areas have been identified as having a role to play in causing depression; no doubt others will be identified in time. It would appear that depression doesn't have one straightforward cause, in the way that diabetes does. Though there is some overlap, your depression may have contributions, directly or indirectly, from one or more of these six areas.

1 Brain chemistry

2 Other illnesses or conditions (include alcohol/drug misuse or addiction)

3 A side-effect of some medications – prescribed or unprescribed

4 Early life

5 Genes

6 Life events, including loss

7 Thinking style

BRAIN CHEMISTRY

Our brain is rather like the 'control' function of a computer; it controls what the body does, including our thinking processes. Each area of the brain controls a different aspect of our bodies. And just like a computer, the settings in our brain should be on a 'default' setting, ready for normal, everyday use. But like a computer, the settings in the brain can change and go wrong. And switching us off and back on won't help! The past 25 years have shown conclusively that when we are depressed, the chemicals used by our brain cells to send messages to each other, called neurotransmitters, are not doing their job properly. The most well-known of these chemical messengers is serotonin.

A major difference between a computer and our brain is that we can easily alter any settings on our computer which have become changed or damaged and are causing malfunctions in what we are trying to do. You can easily reset the default printer, alter the volume, the colour on screen, or which wi-fi to connect to. But we can't do that with our brain if something's gone amiss. How strange, but useful, would it be if we could?

Instead, we have to use the most common equivalent for the human brain, and that is medication. Most modern medications for depression are designed to increase the levels of the neurotransmitter serotonin in the brain (see also chapters 4 and 9). This kind of targeted medication is still in its infancy, having become available only in the past 20 years, and I'm sure each decade will bring new developments to improve the effectiveness of antidepressants and other techniques for treating mood regulation.

OTHER ILLNESSES OR CONDITIONS

When you first begin to feel depressed, often your first thought is that you're just imagining it. After a few more days, you're sure it's not all in your mind, and you start to look for a reason. Work difficulties? Relationship difficulties? Must be something.

But sometimes depression can follow an illness or be an effect of another medical condition that you have. The depression might be directly due to the other illness, or it might be the lifestyle change and distress caused by that illness which triggers depression. This is more common than is realized and it is worth excluding the possibility before considering what to do next. For example, if you have become depressed since being diagnosed with cancer or heart disease or you've had a stroke, you may find that approaching a support group for people with similar experiences would be particularly helpful for you, as they will have experience of being where you are now.

In my own case, I'd had a severe bout of glandular fever that nearly caused me to be hospitalized, and was so ill that I was in bed for several weeks. I discovered much later that the several years of severe depression that began shortly afterwards was probably triggered by that illness. Illnesses and conditions which are associated with depressive illness, occurring either with or after the illness, include:

- flu
- glandular fever
- head injury
- alcohol misuse or addiction
- stroke
- long, painful illnesses like arthritis
- lupus
- ulcerative colitis
- diabetes
- AIDS
- Wilson's disease
- multiple sclerosis
- Parkinson's disease
- heart disease
- underactive thyroid.

Quick fix

Wrap up the love you receive today and keep it safe in your heart for when you need its strength and warmth to keep you going.

A SIDE-EFFECT OF SOME MEDICATIONS

Depression is a known side-effect of many prescribed medications. Always check the leaflet that comes with your medication for details of side-effects; and check again at intervals, as manufacturers can make changes to a drug or discover a new side-effect. With some illnesses, it's difficult to be sure whether it is the ailment or the medication which is having the depressive effect. Typical examples of medications which can be associated with depression include:

▶ Beta-blockers

▶ some steroids

▶ Antabuse (for alcohol addiction)

▶ some sleeping pills

▶ statins (for high cholesterol)

▶ Levodopa (for Parkinson's disease)

▶ Accutane (for acne)

▶ some hormones (the pill, or for symptoms of menopause)

▶ Zovirax (for herpes or shingles).

Point to remember

If you suspect that your low mood is an outcome of medication, prescribed or over the counter, or of recreational or other drug use (e.g. alcohol or cannabis can both cause depression), you should discuss this with your doctor or pharmacist, who should be able to offer advice. **It's very important that you don't reduce or stop taking your prescribed medication without speaking to your doctor.**

EARLY LIFE EXPERIENCES

When I was depressed, I found my thoughts often turned to my childhood, and because my mood was low and negative, this tended to throw up long-forgotten hurts and disappointments. This happens to many people who are depressed. Sometimes these memories can be so painful that it's easy to feel that they are the cause of the way you are currently feeling. And sometimes this is true. Studies have consistently shown that emotional neglect and a lack of attention, empathy and support from carers is linked with depression in later life. Losing a parent through separation or death before the age of about 11 can particularly increase your susceptibility to depression in adult life.

Point to remember

It's important to consider these remembered childhood experiences carefully, however, because there are two processes which could be occurring.

* Being depressed tends to encourage all the negative thoughts, memories etc to come to the forefront of your thoughts, and makes you want to chew over it again and again. This is a symptom of being depressed. But if you had a fairly balanced and ordinary childhood, continuing such ruminations can give undue importance to problematic childhood experiences you may have had that were in reality an occasional blip in an otherwise contented childhood.

* If you were unfortunate enough to have had a childhood that was disadvantaged and experienced neglect or ill treatment, your mind will be working its way through this old business you have. If you find that you often remember and relive distressing times from your early life or have upsetting dreams, you might want to talk to your doctor to find out if counselling might be helpful for you.

GENES

My maternal grandfather was colour blind, although my mother was not. My brother is colour blind, but his daughter is not, although her son is. Our family's pattern of colour blindness – the way it skips generations and is mainly acquired by boys from mothers who are carriers of the gene – encapsulates the parts that inheritance and genetics can play in our lives.

Just like colour blindness, a tendency to be of low mood and become depressed is inherited. Unlike colour blindness, it's a tendency or vulnerability to depression that's passed on, not the condition itself. A family tendency doesn't mean you will definitely have depression. There has to be a trigger or set of circumstances that bring this out. Many people with the tendency go through their whole lives unaffected and unaware of it, or it may show itself in different ways in different people, perhaps as a phobia, OCD, panic attacks or anxiety.

Your thinking space

Think about your blood relatives.

✳ Do you have any close family members who have been anxious or depressed, or had panic attacks, social phobia, agoraphobia or OCD?

✳ What about aunts, uncles, grandparents or great-grandparents?

✳ Sometimes depression in older generations showed itself differently from today. Did you have an aunt or uncle who was a bit eccentric or was a recluse? Or anyone who was described as frail or poorly, and didn't go out much or attend family functions?

LIFE EVENTS, INCLUDING LOSS

Experiences that can trigger depression often involve a loss of some kind. Maybe someone close has died, or your life has changed in a major way. But this kind of loss or change won't trigger depression in everyone. It's depends how we deal with it. If you experience a feeling of grief or loss and don't or can't acknowledge it and talk about it, those feelings turn inwards, and can deepen and intensify until in time they can show on the outside as depression. It would be difficult to list everything that we can lose in life, but here are some common examples:

▶ bereavement

▶ loss of a pet

▶ new job

▶ moving home

▶ menopause

▶ retirement

▶ loss of a physical or mental ability through illness or an accident

▶ children leaving home

▶ redundancy

▶ growing older

- before or after childbirth

- a relationship ending.

In many ways, a bereavement can be straightforward to deal with, as others around you are likely to be feeling the same sense of grief, and there are many opportunities to express your feeling of loss. This is not always the case, however. If for some reason you haven't had an opportunity to express grief, or haven't felt able, this may show up later as depression.

But most life events and life changes have more variable reactions, and it can be difficult to even acknowledge your feelings if everyone around you is excitedly looking forward to starting at university, or can't wait to move to that new home or for the children to grow up, yet you don't feel like that at all. Yes, you welcome the new experiences, challenges and opportunities, but there's also a feeling in the pit of your stomach that's tinged with regret and loss at what you'll be leaving behind. The irony is that many of those around us are doing just what we are doing – putting on a happy face and pretending to be immune to these losses. So if you feel it and can't express it, find someone you can talk to about it, such as an understanding relative, friend or colleague, or a trusted mentor or adviser.

Mythbuster

Myth: Depression only affects people who aren't strong enough to cope with life's difficulties.

Truth: Depression can happen to absolutely anyone, from the high-powered executive to the check-out assistant, and from your doctor to the school cleaner.

THINKING STYLE

This is a bit of chicken-and-egg cause. It's hard to say which came first, the depression or the thinking style. Probably a bit of each. Chapter 5 covers thinking styles in more details, but here are examples of people whose thinking habits tend to pull down their mood.

Maya, Portsmouth

> ...always blames herself if a relationship fails. In her head, she goes over and over all the things she should have done differently and that must have caused the break-up. She thinks she's got lots of faults, and tries so hard to sort them out. But it never occurs to her that some of the fault may lie with her partner, not her, or that some people are just not meant for each other.

Chris, Chelmsford

> ...hates his new job. He likes the work, and was so pleased to get this job, but he thinks his team don't like him. They just get on with their work, and apart from in meetings, don't talk to him much. It's really getting him down. But Chris never thinks to wonder why this might be, and that it might be nothing to do with him. The team may have been pulled up recently by their line manager for spending too much time chatting, or they may be working on a very tight schedule.

Emma, Birmingham

> ...is a perfectionist. She likes to do everything just right. Organized and just so. Takes pride in it. But when she and partner Scott have their first child, she just can't cope with the unpredictability of it all, and trying to maintain her punishing standards at home and at work. Having very high standards works well in a few situations, like analysing blood samples in a hospital, but in most of what we do, aiming for perfection will be a pipe dream which will bring constant disappointment.

Mythbuster

Myth: Depressed people are mainly sad, self-centred people.

Truth: Sad they may be, but no more likely to be self-centred than anybody else.

Next steps

The key points covered in Chapter 3 are:

* even rich and famous people get depressed
* are some people more likely to become depressed than others?
* depression and older people
* depression and children
* coping with difficult times of year.

3

Who gets depressed?

Who gets depressed? The answer is that anybody can become depressed.

And it's not just everyday people. Celebrities from actor Harrison Ford to former Spice Girl Mel C have been depressed. Even famous historical figures such as the artist Claude Monet and the poet John Keats experienced depression.

No matter how rich, successful and famous you are, you can still become depressed. Money doesn't bring with it immunity to feeling down. Feelings of depression are not confined to causes such as poverty, poor housing or unemployment, as we saw in Chapter 2.

But although anyone can become depressed, are there some people who are more likely to experience it?

How do you feel?

1 From your experience, would you say that depression is:

   a Quite common
   b Rare
   c Very common
   d Not sure/Don't know

2 From the people you know, which of these seems to be true?

   a More women become depressed than men.
   b More men become depressed than women.
   c Don't know.

3 Thinking about the people you know, which age group or groups would you say are most likely to be depressed? (Choose all that apply.)

   a Teenagers
   b Those aged 20–60
   c People over 60
   d Not sure/Don't know

4 Thinking about yourself or another person you know who has depression, are you aware of anything which may have caused it?

5 Which of these makes you more likely to feel down or depressed? (Choose all that apply.)

   a Being on your own
   b People coming to visit
   c Christmas or New Year
   d Bank holidays
   e Dark winter days.

Greater openness

Until recently, the rich and famous would be likely to hide behind a mask of health and well-being, projecting an image of happiness and contentment. Any suggestion that they could feel down and depressed, or anxious and stressed like the rest of us was entirely out of the question, and they would go to great lengths to maintain that image.

It's hard to say when the mask began to slip, but it came off completely during the break-down of the marriage of the Prince of Wales and Diana, Princess of Wales in the 1990s. Intimate details of the princess's bulimia and her struggle to cope with her life in the public eye came into the public domain with the publication of Andrew Morton's biography of her. Suggestions of depression and suicide attempts also became public. None of this was disputed by the princess. Although the reasons for the Andrew Morton biography were nothing to do with being more open about mental health issues, the publication of the book and the ensuing media and public interest probably heralded a sea change in how celebrities behave when they are experiencing psychological difficulties such as stress, anxiety or depression, or are misusing alcohol or drugs.

The growing number of celebrities who have openly talked about their experience of depression includes Alastair Campbell, Drew Barrymore, Sting, Woody Allen, John Cleese, Robbie Williams, Eminem, Jack Dee, George Michael, Sheryl Crow, Billy Joel, Britney Spears and Owen Wilson. It is now almost an everyday occurrence to hear of another celebrity wrestling with a psychological problem and seeking therapy. At one time none of these celebrities would have risked being so open about such problems, so it's refreshing to see that the stigma attached to depression has lessened. However, it can still be difficult for non-celebrities to be so open, at work or with friends and family.

Case study: Susan Boyle

Sometimes we see a celebrity reacting badly to a stressful situation, and then hear of them going for help in a clinic. A recent example is Susan Boyle, who became a worldwide star overnight in 2009, after an astonishing audition for *Britain's Got Talent*, which was subsequently viewed by millions on YouTube. When, some weeks later, she failed to win the talent competition, coming second instead, her humiliation was broadcast live on TV, and it was not a surprise that this vulnerable lady required treatment in the days that followed. Susan's slight learning difficulties made such life-changing events even harder to cope with. Fortunately, she received the support and treatment she needed, returned to good health, and currently continues to cope well with worldwide fame.

Quick fix

If you have a willing friend or partner, a scalp or shoulder and neck massage can help to relax your entire body. Start slowly with gentle, short, broad strokes, using flattened fingers, to warm up the whole area to be massaged. Then, still with flat fingers, use slow, gliding strokes and light to medium pressure to release tension. If the pressure could just crush a ripe grape under your fingers, you've got it about right.

Sex variations

As mentioned in Chapter 1, the NHS estimated in 2012 that 25 per cent of women and 10 per cent of men in the UK will require treatment for depression at some point in their lives. It is suggested that women are more affected because of the particular lifestyles women have, such as juggling home and work, being a single parent or caring for elderly relatives – and sometimes all of these at once. Also, the normal stages of women's lives involve continual hormonal upheaval: the menstrual cycle, pregnancy, the post-pregnancy period, infertility, menopause, and the possibility of being childless. All of these events can bring wide variations in emotions and moods that can trigger depression for some women. This pattern of a higher incidence of depression in women is found worldwide.

However, although overall more women than men are depressed at any time, this isn't the same for all age groups. A 2001 survey of the UK found that:

▶ depression for women peaks at age 55–59

▶ depression for men is at its highest at age 45–49.

According to a 2001 survey of the UK, the ages at which more men or more women are likely to be depressed are:

Age range	More women depressed	More men depressed
16–19	√	
20–24	√	
25–29		√
30–34	√	
35–39	√	
40–44		√
45–49		√
50–54	√	
55–59	√	
60–64		√
65–69	√	
70–74	√	

Case study: Roberto

Roberto couldn't wait for his last day at work. He worked in the fish market in London, and his 65th birthday was rapidly approaching. How wonderful it would be not to have to get up and go out so early in the morning. His retirement came before he knew it. They gave him a great send-off on the day! Then, it had arrived: retired life. And how great it was. Walking with Ellie. Getting all the jobs about the house done. But then the days began to feel too long. And his energy tailed off, and everything was an effort. He'd never felt so low in his life. Roberto wondered what on earth was wrong with him? Ellie told him that adjusting to retirement takes time, and suggested they attend a 'Preparing for retirement' event. She knew, she'd just been through the experience herself.

Mythbuster

Myth: Being depressed is something people choose to be. They've just given in.

Truth: Not! Thousands of people who have been depressed will tell you different.

Vulnerable groups

There are many people in the UK and elsewhere who, through no fault of their own, are more likely to develop a mental health problem, with depression being one of the most common. A 2007 report on Great Britain by the Mental Health Foundation found that the risk of developing depression was increased by various factors.

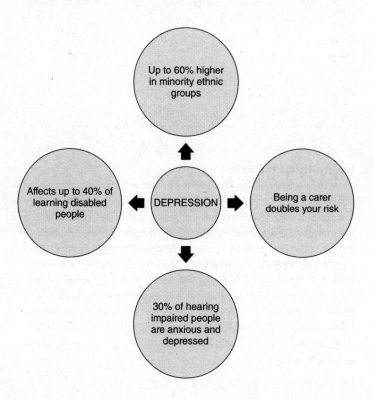

Up to 60% higher in minority ethnic groups

Affects up to 40% of learning disabled people

DEPRESSION

Being a carer doubles your risk

30% of hearing impaired people are anxious and depressed

Quick fix

Change your routine a bit. The same schedule, places, people, sounds and smells can become associated with the same feelings of anxiety or depression. So gradually make a few changes.

Children

It used to be thought that children couldn't be depressed because they weren't emotionally capable of it. But this belief has now been overturned. As children, boys and girls are equally likely to be affected, with the BBC website (2012) giving a figure of at least 20 per 1,000 children under 12 being affected. By the teenage years this increases to 50 in 1,000. More general material about recognizing and helping children with depression is given in Appendix 3.

Quick fix

Count how many times you breathe out in a minute.

Now, do the same thing again.

The second number should be lower than the first, and you should now feel more relaxed.

The over 65s

Reported rates of depression indicate that these fall in the over 65s for both men and women. But there is general acceptance that this is not a true representation. Age Concern reports that rates of depression continue to increase with age. This inconsistency has a number of causes. One could be that the methods used to assess depression in the over 65s may not be suited to this age group. Another is that older people often do not recognize that they are depressed, putting such feelings down to their life circumstances. Perhaps they've lost their partner, or some old friends. Or maybe they have difficult neighbours, or mobility isn't what it used to be.

The Mental Health Foundation's 2007 report also showed the factors increasing depression in this age group.

Mythbuster

Myth: Depressed people are just full of self-pity.

Truth: I felt many things when I was depressed – bewilderment, anger, guilt, helpless, useless, lost – but self-pity was not one of them. There was no room left for self-pity.

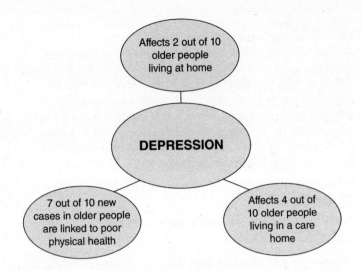

Affects 2 out of 10 older people living at home

DEPRESSION

7 out of 10 new cases in older people are linked to poor physical health

Affects 4 out of 10 older people living in a care home

Adversity and depression

Chapter 2 gave the seven main causes of depression. Three of these – illness, early life and life events (including loss) – taken together, can be thought of as the 'adversity' we've been subjected to in our life. Adversity of many kinds can make people of any age and any background more vulnerable to depression. But there's nothing inevitable about this process. Other factors will determine whether you experience depression or not.

First, there's an element of chance about whether or not you become depressed. Even if you have inherited a genetic tendency, it is not definite that you will become depressed. If your life path doesn't take you through the kind of adversity that might trigger depression, you'll live your life unaware of what might have been and the luck you have had. Millions of people do just that.

Your thinking space

According to the Mental Health Foundation's report (2007), these are some of the adverse situations, or triggers, which can make depression more likely. Do any of these apply to you?

* ✳ Lack of control over your life
* ✳ Sexual abuse in childhood
* ✳ War and conflict
* ✳ Poverty
* ✳ Natural disasters
* ✳ Long hours at work
* ✳ Difficult times of year
* ✳ Overloaded at work
* ✳ Difficult line manager
* ✳ Loss, disappointment or bereavement
* ✳ A failure or disappointment
* ✳ Bullying
* ✳ Living in a very remote area which is also an area of deprivation.

Your personal journal

Turn to a page at the back of your journal and put at the top the heading 'Information or ideas I find helpful'. As you are working through the book, when you find a particularly helpful idea, thought or explanation, make a note of it here, along with the page it was on. Alternatively, you can underline or highlight the text.

Resilience to depression

Adversity may make us vulnerable to depression, but resilience can reduce that vulnerability. Developing ways of improving resilience to depression is currently the subject of many research projects.

I would suggest that this kind of resilience can come from characteristics such as:

- a positive attitude to life

- an excellent support network

- inner strength, self-esteem and self-respect

- your personality

- your ability to think about and solve problems

- knowing how and when to relax

- being willing to make an effort for something you want

- feeling you have control over what happens to you.

Although some of the items on this list will be outside your control, most are qualities you can work on to build your resilience. You'll find suggestions on how to do this in every chapter, and particularly Chapter 11, which looks at building resilience to stress. Stress of one kind or another is very often the trigger for depression.

Mythbuster

Myth: Coming through depression makes you stronger.

Truth: Everyone reacts differently to being depressed, and recovering from it. There are no hard and fast rules. I feel my inner self has been hurt by the experience of depression and is now more sensitive than it would otherwise have been. But my outer shell has acquired Teflon-strong armour to protect me from future hurt.

Next steps

The key points covered in Chapter 4 are:
* **what to expect when you go to your doctor**
* **the kinds of treatment you may be offered**
* **the people who know how to help you**
* **how you can help yourself.**

Types of treatment

When I was depressed, I was in my early twenties, and treatment options for depression were limited. Early medications weren't very effective and most had serious side-effects, while talking treatments were hard to find. I mostly used self-help because that's all that was easily available. But in the few decades since then, there have been huge steps forward in developing better drugs and creating effective talking treatments. This chapter will discuss these and some other treatments.

I'll also explain the range of professionals who work with people who are depressed, and clarify the differences between them. And don't forget that it's not only the professionals who can play an important part in your recovery, but also partners, friends, family and you yourself. A one-size-fits-all approach doesn't work when it comes to treating depression. We're all different, and you need the right treatment or the right combination of treatments for you.

How do you feel?

1 How much would you say you know about treatments for depression?

   a A little
   b Nothing
   c Quite a lot
   d As much as I can

2 How many treatments for depression are you aware of?

   a Just medication
   b Medication and one other treatment
   c More than one treatment
   d None

3 Thinking about medication for depression, what has been your experience of it? (Choose any that apply.)

   a Good
   b Average
   c Not good
   d Have never been prescribed medication
   e Have been prescribed medication, but didn't take it

4 Thinking about 'talking treatment' for depression, i.e. talking to a health professional other than your doctor over a number of sessions, what has your experience been?

   a I've never been offered 'talking treatment'
   b I've been offered 'talking treatment', but didn't accept
   c Good
   d Average
   e Not good

5 Thinking about any other kinds of treatment for depression (not medication or talking treatment), what has your experience been? (Choose any that apply.)

   a I'm not aware of any other treatments
   b I've not been offered any
   c I've thought about them, but never tried any
   d Good
   e Average
   f Not good.

A wide choice

We are used to taking medication or having other kinds of treatment if the doctor says we should. This might be having antibiotics for an infection, physiotheraphy for a strained muscle, stitches for a deep cut, plaster on a broken wrist etc. We know where we are with these kinds of treatment.

But with depression, it's different. There isn't one universally agreed, tried-and-tested form of treatment. Also, we all bring to this subject the views about the different treatments that we've built up through our own experiences, those of people we know and magazine articles, documentaries or internet reports we may have seen.

Being depressed makes it difficult to make choices. It can also make you feel you don't matter, and that it's not worth trying to get better. Finding the energy and clear thinking needed to make a choice can be hard, and you can easily end up not doing anything. Reading this book will help you to cut through all of this and find your way forward. This chapter is intended to help you through the maze to some clear answers.

There is helpful information throughout the book, more detailed information in the appendices and contact details for further sources of information in Appendix 4. If you don't feel up to exploring this yourself at present, ask a trusted friend or loved one to do it for you. Those close to you often don't know what to say or how to help, and they will be only too pleased to do something that will help you to get better. Here are some ways you, or a supportive friend, can find help or learn more for yourself.

▶ Talk to your doctor, practice nurse or health visitor.

▶ Talk to the pharmacist.

▶ Obtain leaflets from your doctor's surgery, pharmacy or health centre.

▶ Read about depression on the internet – but make sure the source is trustworthy and covers the main points (see Appendix 4 for links to good sites).

▶ Find a local self-help group.

▶ Check at your local library, as many have a well-stocked section, sometimes called a 'bibliotherapy' section, with information about problems such as depression, stress and anxiety.

Reasons to have treatment

You may wonder what would happen if you didn't go for treatment. And the answer probably isn't what you would expect. Research has found that even without being treated, most people with depression will gradually get better by themselves. That's why an older relative or friend might have told you they were depressed years ago, before much was known about it, and that they just soldiered on, and then one day they realized the depression had gone and they felt better. So why get treated?

It may not seem obvious at first, but suppose you tripped and fell, and cut your face on some broken glass. It's a deep cut and needs two or three stitches. If you leave the cut untreated, it will probably get better on its own, but this could take a long time and you would be left with a permanent scar. There is also the risk that the cut could become infected, making you very ill for weeks and producing a more ugly scar. It's easy to forget, in these days of free healthcare and antibiotics, that many simple health problems, if left untreated, can become much more complex and even life-threatening. Depression is just the same. I know a number of women whose post-natal depression was not treated, and they struggle with recurring bouts of depression.

There are at least ten good reasons for being treated.

1 You'll get better much sooner.

2 The depression is likely to be less severe.

3 You're less likely to need time off work.

4 You're less likely to have depression again.

5 You're less likely have mental scars.

6 You're less likely turn to drugs or alcohol to feel better.

7 Some depression, especially mild depression, can go on for a long time and this is less likely with treatment.

8 You're less likely to develop a more severe depression.

9 You're less likely to attempt suicide.

10 It will be much easier on you and on those around you.

Taking the first step

If you think you may be depressed, seeing your doctor is usually the first point of contact. It can be difficult to go and see your doctor if you're depressed, but doctors see people with depression every day, and you can talk to your doctor about anything. Some doctors have more expertise in this area than others, so you can try another member of the practice to compare what's available to you. The doctor may refer you to another professional who can provide more specialist treatment.

Although the range of treatments which can help depression will be described, bear in mind that what is actually available to you will probably depend on where you live, unless you can afford to be treated privately. Medication can be prescribed anywhere, but a 'talking treatment' is currently easier to find in urban areas and in south-east England than elsewhere, giving people in those area more choice.

The National Institute for Health and Clinical Excellence (NICE) issues guidelines on the treatment of depression. In its 2009 report, the Institute suggested a three-stage approach, and it is these guidelines that your doctor will follow at your first visit when considering what treatment to offer to you. Here is an outline of what you might expect.

Mild to moderate depression

Medication is not often prescribed for mild depression because mild depression can go away without treatment, and for some people the side-effects will outweigh the benefits. Doctors encourage a 'wait and watch' approach, and will ask you to see them regularly. They may suggest guided self-help or short-term talking treatments and exercise programmes.

Severe depression

If the depression is more severe, the doctor will probably recommend antidepressants, and in particular a type called selective serotonin reuptake inhibitors (SSRIs), which are less likely to cause problematic side-effects than other types of antidepressants.

Combining a talking treatment with SSRI medication can be the most effective treatment for severe depression, so you may also be offered one of the talking treatments.

Severe depression which is resistant to therapy

If your depression is severe, proving resistant to any kind of therapy and there is a risk to life or of self-neglect, the treatment will be a combination of medication with a more in-depth talking therapy. In-patient care would also be considered to ensure your general well-being and safety.

If it's important to relieve this kind of depression quickly, a treatment known as electro-convulsive therapy (ECT) would be considered (this is explained later in this chapter).

Types of treatment

MEDICATION

The treatment for depression which people are most familiar with is medication, in the form of antidepressants. Several types of antidepressant have been developed in the past 50 years, some more successful than others. Chapter 9 is devoted to the various medications used for depression, explaining how they work, the side-effects, and the best way to come off medication.

Point to remember

Who can prescribe antidepressants?

Only a medical doctor can prescribe antidepressants. All psychiatrists are medical doctors. The majority of qualified psychologists are not medical doctors, although they may use the prefix 'Dr': this refers to their doctorate in psychology.

TALKING TREATMENTS

Your doctor may be able to offer you one of a range of psychological, or talking, treatments. The term 'talking treatment' was coined to distinguish this way of dealing with depression from taking medication. Your choice of talking treatment will depend on what's available, your own preferences, how severe your depression is and a number of other factors dealt with later in this chapter. In some areas, there may be a waiting list for these therapies. If you have healthcare insurance this kind of help can be accessed more quickly.

It can be very hard to talk about your private experiences, but healthcare professionals understand this and will put you at ease. The sessions are also your opportunity to ask them any questions you have about your condition.

Here are some of the key styles of talking treatment which may be available to you in the UK on the NHS.

▶ Cognitive behavioural therapy (CBT) is the most likely treatment to be offered. It can help you become aware of the negative thoughts and thinking styles that are part of depression, and show you how you could replace these. It typically consists of a one-hour session with the therapist at fortnightly or monthly intervals for up to 12 months.

▶ In some areas, a computerized version of cognitive behaviour therapy (CCBT) can be accessed at your doctor's surgery or online. NICE recommends a programme called 'Beating the Blues' to treat mild to moderate depression.

▶ Five or six sessions of problem-solving therapy can help you to break down problems to manageable proportions and develop strategies for coping with them.

▶ Family therapy can be offered when issues and relationships within the family are relevant to your depression.

▶ Loss/bereavement counselling.

▶ General counselling gives you the chance to talk over feelings and concerns with an objective and supportive professional, who will listen to you with empathy and acceptance. This gives you the space to mull everything over and find your own solutions. Many doctor's practices have counsellors on-site, with little, if any, waiting time.

▶ Guided self-help delivers a six- to eight-week therapy programme through self-help books under the guidance of a healthcare professional. This is sometimes called 'bibliotherapy', and may be based at your local library.

Quick fix

Start to believe in yourself. Just a tiny bit. Whatever you can manage now will be just great.

Cognitive behavioural therapy

Cognitive behavioural therapy (CBT) sounds more complicated than it is. It's probably easier to tell you what CBT is *not*.

▶ You will not lie on a couch or sit in a big leather chair and just talk.

▶ The therapist will not sit behind a big desk and say nothing while you do all the talking.

▶ Your childhood and sex-life will not be analysed.

▶ Sessions will not be with a psychiatrist.

▶ Just talking to the therapist during the sessions will not make you better.

▶ Therapy will not take at least a year.

Here is what *will* happen.

▶ The therapist might be a psychologist, a nurse or a specially trained counsellor or other health professional.

▶ You and the therapist will work as a team.

▶ Most discussion will be about the 'here and now', not the past.

▶ You'll mainly be working on finding ways to improve your everyday thoughts and daily life.

▶ You may have some questionnaires and other straightforward activities to work on between sessions.

- You'll understand what you're doing and why.

- You'll learn everyday coping skills, such as how to relax, how to challenge worrying or negative thoughts, how to think in ways which make depression less likely.

- Treatment is likely to involve 16–20 one-hour sessions spread over three to four months, with the possibility of a further monthly session for up to six months.

The name of 'cognitive behavioural therapy' was adopted after two existing successful therapies were combined: cognitive therapy and behaviour therapy.

Cognitive therapy works from the viewpoint that how we see situations influences how we react emotionally to them. So certain ways of thinking can cause symptoms such as depression or anxiety. This kind of thinking has been called 'distorted thinking'. Becoming aware of these distorted thoughts and then challenging and changing them can lessen feelings of depression.

Behaviour therapy aims to weaken the connection which has been made between situations and unhelpful emotional reactions to them, such as anxiety or depression. This allows you to regain control of your behaviour and make the changes you want.

CBT works on the principle that we all learn unhelpful ways of thinking and behaving over a period of time: bad habits, as it were. If we can become aware of these thoughts and understand how they can be problematic to our feelings and behaviours, then we can learn how to challenge negative ways of thinking, and this can bring about more positive feelings and the changes in behaviour that we want. CBT focuses on the present and breaks problems into smaller parts to make them easier to deal with. Chapters 5 and 6 will explain this more fully.

Point to remember

CBT combines two very effective forms of therapy: cognitive therapy and behavioural therapy.

OTHER TREATMENTS
Electro-convulsive therapy

Electro-convulsive therapy (ECT) is a medical treatment that has been used since the 1930s for a number of psychiatric conditions. It is a very effective treatment, but it is also controversial and is only used when someone is severely depressed and hasn't responded to other treatment, particularly if medication is having little or no effect, or they are at high risk of seriously harming themselves. The Scottish ECT Accreditation Network (SEAN) report of an audit of all ECT clinics in Scotland in 2010, concluded that in three-quarters of cases, people with depressive illness showed 'a definite improvement' immediately after ECT.

The reason for the controversy is that ECT involves passing a small electric current across the brain, and this produces a seizure (a fit or convulsion). The procedure is painless, as the patient is sedated or under a general anaesthetic. It is thought that it is the seizure which lifts the depression, but there is still no agreement about how ECT works, although it may be that it alters the brain's response to its chemical messengers, the neurotransmitters.

Typically, treatment requires two or three sessions a week, over two weeks or a month, and it can be very effective, especially for the most difficult cases. However, it's not a pleasant experience, and it can have serious side-effects, including a headache immediately after each treatment and some temporary memory loss.

I had ECT as a last resort for my depression, which had not improved at all with medication, and I experienced both of those side-effects. However, though the experience was strange and unpleasant, it did have a remarkable effect on my depression. I only had two sessions, but following the first one, my depression lifted like a curtain and it was as if the sun had come out again in my life; colours were brighter and more vibrant. It was as if I was Dorothy in the 1939 film of *The Wizard of Oz*, firstly because my world changed from black and white into colour, as the film does, and secondly because my world seemed to have returned to the safe and friendly place it used to be, like Dorothy's does at the end of the film.

Transcranial magnetic stimulation

Transcranial magnetic stimulation is a new treatment that has only been available for a few years. Although not useful for everyone, this treatment is very effective for those it does help. It may be tried in cases of severe depression when other treatments have failed. The equipment is positioned outside the head, with little contact, no pain and no need for a general or local anaesthetic. The small coil of wire which produces the magnetic field is positioned next to the scalp so that it stimulates the nerve cells in the brain that are involved in depression. Each treatment lasts 40 minutes, and about 30 treatments are needed over a six-week period. It looks similar to having a tooth X-ray at the dentist, but it should be safer than an X-ray, as it is a magnetic field which is passed into the brain.

At the time of writing, NICE has not expressed any safety concerns about the procedure. However, NICE recommends that until the best possible procedure for the treatment has been developed, it should only be used in research studies.

Light therapy

If you have seasonal affective disorder (SAD), depression only appears in the winter months, and you should find that light therapy can produce a dramatic improvement. A special light box or lamp can replace the sunshine your brain is missing if you sit in front of it for several hours each day during the winter months. A dawn simulator light, which increases in brightness gradually, can also be helpful in the mornings.

But light therapy isn't just for people with SAD. Lack of light can affect anyone, as the changing seasons and length of day help to set our body clock and various biological rhythms, such as hormone levels, appetite, energy levels and sleepiness. If you go to work in the dark and come home in the dark, or you spend long hours away from natural daylight, these 'circadian rhythms' get out of sync.

This can cause problems such as overeating, poor appetite, insomnia, feeling tired all the time (TATT) or pre-menstrual syndrome (PMS).

Types of professionals

With this variety of therapies and support available, it is important that the professional concerned has the training and experience to support and guide you. If you have any concerns or questions about what you're being offered, or the background of the person who will be working with you, talk it over with your doctor or the therapist before proceeding. Likewise, if you have had several sessions with a therapist and you just don't feel the relationship between you is working, talk to the therapist or, if you prefer, to your doctor about your concerns. Such situations are not unusual in talking therapies and it's common to change therapists. It's not seen as a complaint or a criticism of the therapist, so you don't have to soldier on. Similarly, a therapist may refer you to a colleague who they think is better able to help you – so don't feel offended if this happens.

So, as well as your doctor, who else is available to help you? What is their training background, and what do they do?

Professional role	Training	Function
Your doctor	Medical training, then training as a general practitioner	Your doctor will diagnose and assess how severe your depression is and offer treatments ranging from 'wait and see' or medication to referral for a talking treatment, exercise programme or bibliotherapy. They should see you regularly to monitor progress.
Clinical psychologist or Counselling psychologist	Clinical and counselling psychologists have a first degree in psychology and at least three years postgraduate study and practice in their specialist area	Clinical psychologists cover all of the clinical applications of psychology. They will use a range of techniques, including CBT for anxious or depressed patients. Counselling psychologists concentrate on using different types of counselling techniques.

Counsellor	A counsellor should have studied and practised counselling for at least two to three years and be a member or accredited member of the British Association of Counselling and Psychotherapy (BACP)	Counsellors work in the short or longer term with people who want to make effective changes to their lives or improve their general well-being. They predominantly 'listen' to you and your 'story', intervening only to help you summarize, weigh up options, discuss past and present life events and emotions, and identify the right course of action for you.
Psychiatrist	A psychiatrist is a medically qualified doctor who has taken at least six further years of training to learn how to help people who have a psychological problem or a mental illness.	In order to assess and diagnose patients, a psychiatrist will discuss your past experiences, family, culture, living environment and work, as well as any relevant medical issues. Your doctor may ask a psychiatrist to be involved in your care if your depression is severe, unresponsive to treatment, there has been difficulty finding a particular medication or where there is uncertainty about a diagnosis.
Community mental health care team		These are locally based teams of 8 to 12 people which bring together all the separate disciplines already described, along with others, such as occupational therapy and social work. This encourages a holistic multi-disciplinary approach and can create an overall care plan for you.
Hospital mental health care team		If your condition merits hospital care or you find yourself in residential care in the NHS or elsewhere, it will normally be a multidisciplinary hospital team, similar to the community mental health team, who will look after you.
Librarian (Bibliotherapy or reading therapy)		It is possible to feel better through reading self-help books or working on self-help workbooks, CDs, DVDs etc. Some libraries and doctor's practices now have a special bibliotherapy area, with specialist books and resources on many aspects of health.
Psychotherapist	Range of backgrounds	Psychotherapy can work with several different approaches, such as CBT, person-centred counselling and psychoanalysis (based on the work of Freud).

Case study: Jack Straw

In autumn 2012, Jack Straw, a former Labour Home Secretary, revealed at the age of 66 that he had had serious depression when he was 33 and had just been elected as an MP. He explained that there were many reasons for this, including a particularly traumatic childhood, the loss of a daughter, difficulties in his new constituency and hearing problems. His mother-in-law recommended seeing a psychotherapist. The one he attended used a psychoanalytical approach, which seemed to suit him, allowing him to cope with his role as an MP over the decades since his treatment.

Point to remember

Professionals involved in working with depressed people must be adequately qualified, and will usually be members of a recognized professional body, such as the Royal College of Psychiatrists or the British Psychological Society. But they must be *full* members, whether that be an accredited member, senior member or fellow. An *associate* membership is usually much easier to achieve, as less experience and training is required, and in some cases just an interest in a subject. So anyone who treats you must be a **full** member of their professional body, not just an associate.

HELP IN YOUR WORKPLACE

Staff in occupational health and welfare departments in workplaces are trained to address the problems of their workforce, including stress and depression. They will treat your case as confidential. Your workplace may have an employee assistance programme which offers free and confidential support off-site for a wide range of problems.

Voluntary groups or charities can help too. In many areas of the UK you can access advice and support for depression through local voluntary groups and charities. Provision tends to be patchy throughout the country, however. Online, there are numerous support groups and discussion groups. It is advisable to check that what is being provided by such organizations is sound before seeking their help (see Appendix 4).

Mythbuster

Myth: Once you're diagnosed with depression, you'll need medication or treatment of some kind for the rest of your life.

Truth: Most people with depression don't need treatment for the remainder of their lives – they are treated for a specific time, and then this finishes.

THE PRIVATE SECTOR

Apart from your doctor, most of what the NHS can provide is also available in the private sector, including in-patient care. Certain types of therapy are only available in the private sector, the most typical examples being alternative and complementary therapies (see Chapter 10), although there are local exceptions to this. See Appendix 4 for details of organizations which provide lists of qualified and regulated therapists.

Here are some guidelines for finding a private counsellor or therapist, or private residential support. If you don't feel up to following any of these suggestions yourself, ask a supportive friend or family member for help – you need to be sure that you are putting yourself in good hands.

▶ Before choosing, make sure you know exactly what service is provided, and don't be afraid to ask precisely what the therapy will involve, how many sessions are needed, and what the cost will be.

▶ Anyone can call themselves a counsellor, psychotherapist or psychologist at present, so you must ensure you find someone with appropriate qualifications and experience. Other terms, however, are protected titles, and it's illegal to use them without the proper qualifications. These include:

  ▷ psychiatrist

  ▷ doctor

  ▷ chartered psychologist

  ▷ clinical psychologist

  ▷ nurse therapist

  ▷ counselling psychologist.

- Never just respond to an advertisement in a newspaper or on the internet. Ask for a recommendation from someone you know who has been successfully treated for depression. Alternatively, ask a therapist for details of at least one satisfied client who would agree to have a chat with you.

- Choose someone who works for a reputable organization, or is a member of a reputable professional body.

- Only agree to treatment from a therapist:

  - who offers the effective treatments you're reading about in this book

  - who has appropriate insurance

  - whose qualifications are accredited by a recognized authority.

- If you decide to work with a therapist or to try an alternative or complementary therapy (ACT), let each therapist or your doctor know what other treatments you're considering, as some of these should not be undertaken at the same time.

Quick fix

How do we know if we are too tense? Begin to notice your muscles. We are usually too busy and preoccupied with other things to notice what our muscles are doing. Think about it now. Focus on the muscles in your fingers, your arms, your shoulders, your back or the back of your neck. Are they relaxed, or do they feel too tense for what you're doing? Then there's your face and forehead. There can be so much tension here. Scan them now. Round your eyes, round your mouth. Your forehead. More tense than they need to be? Start today to notice these things. Become more self-aware.

Help from partners, friends and family

No matter what treatment plan you are on, when you are down, some friendly and supportive company can give you a huge boost. A chat and a cuppa or a trip to the shops or the park can break up a long dull day. Isn't it funny how some of your friends and family seem to just know what to say and do to make you feel better, while others make you want to crawl back to bed and hide. Yes, it matters what your friends, family and loved ones say and how they react to you. If you have a friend or loved one who is depressed and you don't know what to say or do, there is helpful information in Appendix 1.

Your depression compass

With so many options for treating or coping with depression, you can find your head is in a spin, especially if you have less energy and poorer concentration and decision-making skills than when you're feeling more yourself. To make this easier, here is a 'compass' to keep you on the right track, just as if you were walking in the hills or the countryside.

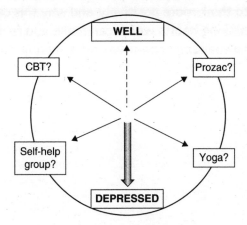

Whatever you do to relieve your depression, and whoever helps you to do this, make sure that you are following these signposts.

▶ Learn how to challenge unhelpful and negative thinking.

▶ Take control and engage with your difficulties.

▶ Remind yourself of your good points and abilities.

▶ Learn how to cope with stress and be more resilient.

▶ Eat healthily and become more active in an enjoyable way.

- Move along at a pace you can cope with – one new thing at a time.

- Use medication if your doctor recommends this, and continue with it for as long as your doctor suggests.

- Use self-help techniques known to be helpful for depression.

- Only see a fully qualified therapist for any treatment.

Next steps

The key points covered in Chapter 5 are:

✳ how your thoughts can affect your mood
✳ what cognitive behavioural therapy and cognitive therapy are
✳ how to think more positively, and why this can help
✳ the thinking habits which can make you feel down
✳ how to challenge negative and worrying thoughts.

Part 2:

Treatments

5

Cognitive behavioural therapy 1: Thinking

Cognitive behavioural therapy (CBT) was introduced in Chapter 4 as one option for treating depression. It's a 'talking therapy', which means you work together with a therapist to explore how you can change your thinking and behaviour in helpful ways. Study after study has shown CBT to be very effective for most people. This chapter will give you an understanding of what to expect of the 'cognitive' part of cognitive behavioural therapy, and what this has to do with treating depression. Chapter 6 will explore how the behavioural aspect of the therapy can benefit people with depression, and what that would mean for you if you choose to have CBT.

How do you feel?

1 How would you describe yourself? (Choose all that apply.)

   a A deep thinker
   b Always thinking about something
   c Can't concentrate on anything
   d Feel my mind is overloaded
   e Can't get my mind off things sometimes

2 How would you describe your thinking most of the time? (Choose one.)

   a Fairly positive
   b Slightly positive
   c Neither positive or negative
   d Slightly negative
   e Fairly negative

3 Thinking about worrying, which of the following would you say apply to you? (Choose all that apply.)

   a I don't worry.
   b I worry sometimes.
   c I tell myself to stop worrying, but it doesn't usually work.
   d I worry all the time.
   e I'm told by other people that I'm a born worrier.

4 Thinking about cognitive behavioural therapy, which of the following would you say apply to you? (Choose any that apply.)

   a I don't know what it is.
   b I have a rough idea what it is.
   c I know what it is.
   d I have tried it and it helped a bit.
   e I have tried it without success.
   f I would like to try it.

5 Which of the following would you say you tend to do? (Choose all that apply.)

   a I jump to conclusions.
   b I see people or situations as either good or bad, with nothing in between.
   c I always think the worst.
   d I blame myself for everything.
   e I focus on the things which didn't go right each day, and forget everything else.

What to expect from CBT

It's worth repeating here the list in Chapter 4 describing what you can expect of CBT. This is because CBT is different from other medical or psychological treatments for depression, and probably different from what you imagine it to be. It is far simpler and less formal than its name suggests.

▶ The therapist might be a psychologist, a specially trained nurse or counsellor, or other health professional.

▶ You and the therapist will work as a team.

▶ The therapist's role is to listen, teach and encourage. Specific techniques and concepts are taught during each session.

▶ Although CBT is known as a 'talking therapy', this is to distinguish it from therapies such as medication or aromatherapy. It isn't 'just talking'. It's talking with a carefully chosen and planned purpose and direction.

▶ The goal of therapy is to learn new ways of reacting, and behaving.

▶ Most discussion will be about the 'here and now', not the past.

▶ You'll mainly be working on finding ways to improve your everyday thoughts and daily life.

▶ Between sessions, you will be reading small amounts of user friendly material, completing questionnaires or diaries, or practising the techniques you've learned. You'll understand what you're doing and why.

▶ You'll learn everyday coping skills, such as how to relax, how to challenge worrying or negative thoughts, how to think in ways which make depression less likely.

▶ Therapists ask questions, and encourage you to ask questions such as, 'How do I really know that those people are gossiping about me? Could they be talking about something else entirely?'

▶ CBT is *non-directive* in the sense that it doesn't tell you how you should feel or what your goals should be. It is *directive* in the sense that you are shown how to think and behave, in ways which will help you reach your goals.

▶ Treatment is likely to involve 16–20 one-hour sessions spread over three to four months, with the possibility of a further monthly session for up to six months.

Mythbuster

Myth: Talking therapy just involves you talking and the therapist listening. What good is that?

Truth: That's an entirely different kind of therapy. Talking therapy for depression is an on-going conversation and interaction between you and the therapist.

What is cognitive therapy?

'Cognitive' is not a word we hear often in everyday conversation, but it is a commonly used term when health professionals talk about the mind and the brain, and how these function. Cognitive therapy is about making changes to your thinking habits and emotional responses in ways that make you feel better about yourself and about your life.

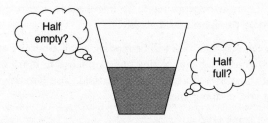

An image often used in cognitive therapy, and one with which most people are familiar, is whether you see a glass as half full or half empty. In other words, do you tend to be happy with what you have or unhappy about what you don't have? This is a good example of what cognitive therapy is about – how different people can perceive the same image or situation in very different ways, and how this in turn leads to a different emotional reaction. Cognitive therapy involves raising a person's awareness of this choice and enabling them to change their thinking to a more positive alternative.

Cognitive therapy was first developed in the 1960s by the American psychiatrist Aaron Beck. It was a fully developed body of knowledge and techniques when it was later joined with behaviour therapy, also already well established, to form CBT, which could then work with people's behaviour as well as their thinking and emotions.

In 1952, long before 'cognitive therapy' had been thought of, the eminent American author Norman Vincent Peale said, 'I change my thoughts, I change my world'. And that is what cognitive therapy helps you to do; it shows you how to change your thoughts, and this has the effect of changing your world for the better. You may not realize it, but how and what you think is not fixed and pre-set. Changing your thoughts is definitely within your control.

Norman Vincent Peale was author of the bestseller *The Power of Positive Thinking*, published in 1952 and still in print today; it has sold more than 20 million copies in more than 40 languages. It was one of the first books on this general subject area which I read, because a supportive friend saw I was struggling and lent it to me. When I saw the title, I was very sceptical, but to my surprise its simple truths and unassuming methods were very powerful. Peale uses Bible passages in places in the book (he was an American pastor), but you can skip these if you prefer and still benefit from the book.

Mythbuster

Myth: Talking things out with a good friend is just as good as 'talk therapy'.

Truth: The term 'talk therapy' came into common usage to distinguish the therapy from medication, which had been the main treatment for depression for many years. The term might make it sound like just having a chat, but it's much more than that. It's talking to a professional specially trained in methods which have been rigorously researched and found to be effective in relieving depression. It also gives you the skills to prevent depression returning. Support from a friend can also be invaluable if you have depression, but professional help will have the surer benefit.

Why we think as we do

Just as we learn how to say 'please', 'thank you' and 'sorry', so we also develop our thinking habits in childhood and in response to our experiences throughout life. As children, we learn from our parents and teachers, but we also pick up ways of thinking and reacting by mirroring those around us – our siblings, neighbours, peers and those we admire. Our thinking and emotional responses are also likely to be significantly affected by our cultural background. A toddler will look around at nearby adults after someone shouts or there's a strange noise outside. The child is waiting to see how the adults react before reacting itself. Is the shouting a good thing or a bad thing? Should I be scared by the noise or find it funny?

It is normal, everyday patterns and habits of thought and belief which can cause a problem in the kinds of situations that people have to deal with in the 21st century. Cognitive therapy works with people over 8–12 sessions to identify exactly how their thinking is causing difficulties for them in their lives. Alternative ways of thinking are then taught, specific to their needs. That being the case, I can only give you examples of the kinds of ideas and new skills which you would work on with your therapist.

Mythbuster

Myth: If you go for talking treatment, it will take years.

Truth: This mistaken view often arises because talking treatment is confused with other types of treatment. A depressed person may go for blocks of six to eight one-hour sessions once a week or fortnight. After a review, this may continue for another one or two blocks if needed.

UNHELPFUL BELIEFS

This has nothing to do with religious or ideological beliefs, but with beliefs which are unhelpful because they are fixed and dogmatic views of the world. If you look closely at these beliefs, though, they are unlikely to be the truth. Holding this kind of belief doesn't mean someone is ill in any way.

Such beliefs are extremely common and entirely 'normal', as we shall see, but they can cause anxiety and depression if you firmly believe them.

Here are some examples. Do you believe any of these to be true?

▶ I should be good at everything.

▶ I need everyone's approval for everything I do.

▶ I should not make a mistake.

Most of these beliefs are opinions that we pick up without noticing it as we're growing up. This is especially the case if praise was rare and criticism of mistakes was more common. It's easy to see how holding one of these beliefs strongly can make life more difficult than it needs to be. And in the longer term this can lead to depression.

Quick fix

If you have something worrying you, try setting aside 15 minutes or so each morning and evening to worry about it. The rest of the time don't allow yourself to think about it at all.

MUSTS AND OUGHTS

All of us have a conversation going on in our heads every day. 'What will we have for dinner?', 'Who is that at the door at this time?', etc. This inner dialogue can sometimes include unhelpful words such as 'ought', 'should' or 'must'. Here are some examples.

▶ I should have done that by now.

▶ I ought to phone him today.

▶ I should tidy that cupboard.

▶ I should have done that better.

These are entirely self-imposed expectations and overly strict personal rules, coming only from yourself. You set these in place in your thinking at some time in your past, probably because of someone else's behaviour, but only you are keeping them going now.

CBT would encourage you to challenge these now by asking yourself, 'Why?' and 'Who says?'. This will help you to adapt your thoughts to something more helpful, such as:

▶ I've been so busy, I haven't finished that yet.

▶ I'd like to phone him today if I can.

▶ I'd like to tidy that cupboard when I have time.

▶ I'd rather have done that better.

Mythbuster

Myth: Talk therapy is exactly the same for everyone.

Truth: Talk therapy is different for everyone, as it is worked out between the therapist and the depressed person.

OTHER UNHELPFUL HABITS

Here are just some of the common thinking errors which can contribute to you feeling anxious or depressed. They are 'errors' in the sense that we are ignoring more positive and more likely explanations in favour of negative conclusions that are much less likely. Some of these thoughts are fairly close in meaning, so there is understandably some overlap.

Thinking error	How it will affect your behaviour
Jumping to conclusions	Expecting, and predicting, that things or people will turn out badly. Other more plausible explanations are ignored. For example, if someone's late, you jump to the conclusion that something awful has happened to them, or that they don't want to see you.
Catastrophizing	Dwelling on the worst possible outcome of an event. If you make a mistake at work, you think the whole project is in jeopardy and you're going to be sacked. You get everything out of proportion.
Personalization	Always blaming yourself for anything negative that happens, with no justification. Whatever goes wrong or doesn't work out, you think that you did something to cause it.
Black and white thinking	Fixed thinking, with two distinct sides and nothing in between – no shades of grey. You see people or events only in black and white, or as good or bad.
Overgeneralization	You believe that if something didn't work out once, it will never work out. So if a relationship ends badly, you think you might as well give up on ever finding a partner.

Your thinking space

Have a look back over the thinking errors in the table above.

Do any of these apply to you? Do any examples come to mind?

Keeping your personal journal

Here's another way you can use your journal as you work through this book. Keep three lists on three separate pages, maybe at the back or centre of your journal:

1 Changes and techniques you're starting *now*
2 Changes and techniques you want to start *soon*
3 Changes and techniques which you'll get to *later*.

Include a page reference with each item to make it easier to refer back to the relevant part of the book.

You can use these journal pages to see how you're doing, and remember what comes next. As time progresses, it's also easy to move items around from *soon* to *now*, or from *later* to *soon* (especially if you use a reusable sticky note for each item).

Challenging unhelpful thinking

People can find that simply becoming aware of unhelpful thinking, along with its effects, can be enough to forge long-lasting change. But often it takes more than that to change, and CBT teaches you how to 'challenge' unhelpful thoughts and beliefs in a way which reduces their negative impact. If you find yourself with an unhelpful thought or belief which is making you feel worried, stressed, anxious or depressed, here's some ideas of how to deal with it.

▶ Use your journal to write things down, or think your way through this process.

▶ Give a rating on a scale of 0 to 100 for how much you believe the unhelpful thought right now.

▶ Now ask yourself these questions; think them through and answer them honestly.

▷ What is the evidence to support this thought?

▷ Who says it's true?

▷ Is it written down somewhere that this is true?

▷ What are the chances of it being true?

▷ Could there be another explanation, that's less upsetting?

▷ What is the evidence supporting the alternative explanation/s?

▷ What would I tell a friend if he or she were in the same situation?

▷ Is there a more realistic and positive thought?

▶ After answering the questions, give a rating between 0 and 100 for how much you believe the unhelpful thought now. With a bit of practice, I would hope that you would find your rating has lowered enough to make you feel less distress.

Quick fix

Whenever you have a negative thought, neutralize it with a positive one. The positive thought doesn't need to be a related thought – anything positive will do. Try it and see.

Don't dwell on things

This advice is about trying to move the mind away from the negative thoughts it's dwelling on and going over and over. This is sometimes called 'ruminating', and people with depression can find this a problem. It's thought that 'ruminating' or dwelling on negative or gloomy thoughts can play a part in keeping depression going. You could think of it as feeding the monster.

Probably the simplest way to switch your attention away from your unwanted thinking is to ring a friend for a chat – not to talk about the stuff that your mind won't let go of, but to chat about something else. Why? Because if you're talking about something else, you can't be thinking about negative stuff at the same time. So to avoid dwelling on things, you could try the following:

▶ phone someone

▶ catch up with your texts

▶ drop by at a neighbour's for a chat, or ask one round

▶ play a game needing concentration, either on your own or with a friend

▶ sing!

▶ play a musical instrument which needs concentration

▶ do anything with other people which involves talking or concentrating on something.

Another good way to occupy your mind is with a mental activity that requires concentration.

▶ Count backwards from 200 in sixes.

▶ List multiples of seven or eight upwards from 0.

▶ Learn a poem or a passage from Shakespeare well enough to recite it. Don't try anything too difficult. Choose something you enjoy or that is funny.

▶ Try to think of boys' or girls' names beginning with every letter of the alphabet. Or an animal, a food, etc.

Finding substitute thoughts

A CBT therapist is likely to ask you to find substitutes for your unhelpful thoughts. Try this for yourself, using your personal journal.

Using a new page in your journal, make two columns, with the headings 'Unhelpful thought' and 'Substitute'. Over the next few days, note down in your journal any 'unhelpful thoughts' that you have. Then work out one or more positive, realistic thoughts that you could substitute for the unhelpful thought, so that you have a less negative emotional response to it.

There's a few here to start you off, with some suggested substitutes.

Unhelpful thought	Substitute
She doesn't care about me.	She was late for our date, but she explained and is usually very loving, so she does care.
	Her job is putting her under pressure right now and she's late for everything. It's not just me.
I'm a bad person.	I may have some bad habits, but I'm definitely not a bad person.
	Lots of people love me so I can't be a bad person.
	Doing a few things I regret doesn't cancel out all the good things I do.
He always lets me down.	He messes up now and then, but most of the time he's there for me.
	He's worried about his exams and it's affecting his concentration.
I should be good all the time.	I don't know anyone else who is good all the time, so why do I need to be?
	I shouldn't apply one set of rules to myself and another set to everybody else.
	Even the best of people do things they regret sometimes.
He is looking at me as if I'm stupid.	He is looking at me, but he could be thinking anything.
	He may be worrying about his job.
	He may not have his contact lenses in.
I can't forgive myself.	Lots of people do things they regret and don't need to forgive themselves to move on.
	As long as I learn something useful from the thing I regret, I don't need to forgive myself to put it behind me and move on.

Quick fix

* Sit comfortably and quietly.
* Close your eyes gently, and become aware of your breathing. Take a gentle breath in and, in your own time, sigh it back out, allowing your shoulders to relax.
* As you breathe in, silently place the word 'slow' on your inward breath and as you breathe out, place the word 'down' on your outward breath.
* Repeat this for 1–2 minutes.

Next steps

The key points covered in Chapter 6 are:

* what behaviour therapy is
* how to actively combat depression
* whether exercise can ease depression
* simple relaxation and breathing exercises which can help
* what panic is and how to cope with panic attacks.

6

Cognitive behavioural therapy 2: Behaviour

In Chapter 6, you'll learn about the 'behavioural' side to cognitive behavioural therapy (CBT). Chapter 5 explained about cognitive therapy, showing how your thinking can affect your mood, and how you can feel better and change your world by changing how you think.

For most people, cognitive therapy is only part of the answer. If behavioural therapy is added to this, the combined effect will be even more powerful. That's what gives cognitive behavioural therapy its strength and effectiveness and its durability. It considers the whole you, and works with you to make straightforward changes which can help to lift depression.

How do you feel?

1 Thinking about behavioural therapy, which of the following would you say applies to you? (Choose any that apply.)

a Don't know what it is
b Have a rough idea what it is
c Know what it is
d Have tried it and it helped
e Have tried it without success

2 When you are feeling well, how active are you most days?

a Not at all active
b Somewhat active
c Quite active
d Very active

3 If you are feeling down or depressed, how active are you most days?

a Not at all active
b Somewhat active
c Quite active
d Very active

4 Which of the following would you say applies to you? (Choose any that apply.)

a Sometimes have feelings of mild panic
b Often have feelings of mild panic
c Never feel any sort of panic
d Sometimes experience acute panic
e Often experience acute panic

5 If you have an everyday problem, what are you most likely to do? (Choose all that apply.)

a Wait and hope it solves itself
b Ask someone else to sort it out
c Ignore it completely
d Deal with it yourself as soon as you can
e Worry about it but do very little.

What is behavioural therapy?

Behavioural therapy aims to work with you to make simple changes to how you behave which will help to lift your mood and make you feel better about you and your life. It does this by focusing on the 'here and now' and teaching new techniques. It doesn't involve telling you what to do or pushing you to do anything. Both cognitive therapy and behavioural therapy emphasize the importance of it being you who makes the decisions. As with cognitive therapy, behavioural therapy is very straightforward and doesn't involve having something done to you; everything you're asked to try will be familiar. It's about showing you what to focus on, and raising your awareness about everyday behavioural changes which can be remarkably effective in relieving depression.

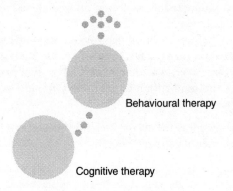

Behavioural therapy

Cognitive therapy

Quick fix

Think about changing what's around you every day. Those familiar sights can become reminders of low mood and negative feelings. So try moving the furniture around, buy a new blind or a new light, tidy a messy corner, throw out some of those old tired ornaments and pictures and buy some bright new ones. Treat yourself to a bunch of cheerful flowers.

Cope better with stress

One aspect of behavioural therapy that is already familiar to most people is stress management. We live in a stressful world and stress is often a trigger for depression, so it is important to know how to recognize when you are stressed and what to do to buffer yourself from the effects. We can do little to influence the major stressors of everyday life, but being able to exercise a degree of control and shield ourselves from its damaging effects is the next best thing. Chapter 11 will show you how to do this in ways which fit easily into your day.

Be as active as you can

According to the NHS website in 2012, there is strong evidence that being active or taking exercise can help people recover from depression, and even prevent them from becoming depressed in the first place. Regular exercise is particularly helpful for mild depression. Staying active makes me feel better in many ways, even when not depressed. The drawback, however, was that when I felt down, finding the energy and momentum to get myself moving was often impossible.

Here are some ideas for overcoming this hurdle, and getting yourself off the sofa and moving.

▶ Start very small – as the saying goes, the longest journey starts with a single step. A walk around the house is good start if it's all you can manage. Then build up from there little by little.

▶ If just getting out of the chair is not easy for you, you can start even smaller. Any sort of movement will be beneficial and make getting out of the chair easier. So try these when you're sitting down:

▷ some craft work that you enjoy, e.g. making cards, painting, tapestry, jewellery-making or sewing with a small sewing machine.

▷ shake your shoulders and arms, and then make fists and punch the air, or do some simple exercises with hand weights.

▷ move about in time to some music.

▷ shake your legs and then do circles with each foot, or other simple exercises.

▷ do the ironing sitting down – just adjust the height of the ironing board.

If you can get up the energy and enthusiasm to *start* doing something, anything at all, you'll quickly feel the benefit. Don't spend time choosing what to do, do anything that will get you moving and feeling better. Just focus on the first step, standing up. Then move on to:

▶ have a shower

▶ do some gardening or housework

▶ re-organize your wardrobe, or your furniture

▶ play a keep-fit DVD or an active computer game.

Enlist a friendly and encouraging companion to join you when you exercise, or just to motivate you to get moving and keep a kindly eye on how you're doing.

Think 'active' rather than 'exercise' – everyday activities such as gardening, cooking, vacuuming, childcare, shopping, walking, etc will all keep you moving until you feel ready for something more.

Point to remember

Choose activities or exercise you really enjoy. Exercise doesn't have to be boring to do you good! Try to find something that fits in easily with your lifestyle – the less effort required the better. Even if you are initially unenthusiastic, the feel-good factor kicks in very quickly, after only five or ten minutes of activity.

The NHS recommended exercise levels below are goals to work gradually towards in the longer term.

Age	Aerobic	Muscle strengthening
5–18	1 hour a day	1 hour on 3 days a week
19 and over	2½ hours a week if moderate*1¼ hours a week if vigorous**	Twice a week, and works all muscle groups

* Moderate exercise means you still have enough breath to talk but you couldn't sing the words to a song.
** Vigorous exercise means you only have enough breath to say a few words.

Aerobic exercise includes such activities as fast walking, cycling, martial arts, running and gymnastics; muscle-strengthening exercise includes activities such as push-ups, gymnastics, hand-held weights and digging the garden.

You don't have to join a gym or exercise to build activity into your life. Here are some ideas for making your days more active even while you're at work or looking after children or other adults.

▶ Walk up the stairs rather than taking the lift whenever you can.

▶ Play with the children – it can help shake off the tiredness at the end of the working day and it's fun too.

▶ At work, walk over to see a colleague in another part of the building, rather than sending an email or phoning.

▶ When out in the car, park a bit further away from your destination and walk the extra distance.

▶ Get off the bus a stop early.

▶ Offer to help with jobs that involve activity.

Exercise releases 'endorphins' in the brain. These brain chemicals have the effect of enhancing your sense of well-being. So choose an activity or exercise that makes you feel good, move forward with care, and you'll find the benefits of regular exercise are very real.

▶ It improves overall health, well-being and general resilience.

▶ It clears and calms your mind.

- It relieves muscle tension.

- It makes you feel less tired.

- It helps you to sleep better.

- It provides refreshing and energizing blood flow around the whole body.

Point to remember

Check with your doctor if you're not sure whether your level of fitness is adequate to begin a particular exercise or activity. If you're new to exercise or haven't exercised for a while, it's best to sign up for a course or join a club so that there's someone available to guide you.

Problem-solving and decision-making

Every day presents us with decisions to make and problems to solve. It's hardly surprising if you sometimes feel swamped by these and put them to one side in the hope that they will miraculously sort themselves out. But burying your head in the sand like this is only putting things off. Eventually, you will have to deal with them. There has to be a better approach to solving problems and making decisions.

The word 'problem' can be used both for 'negative' problems and 'positive' problems.

'Negative' problems:

- I've lost my train ticket.

- I can't pay my bills.

- I have an appraisal at work tomorrow.

- I owe my friend £50 and I can't pay it back. He wants it now.

- I can't seem to get a job.

- My floorboards were damaged when I had a gas leak.

'Positive' problems:

▶ What shall I buy with my birthday money?

▶ Where shall we go on holiday?

▶ My best friend wants me to go on holiday with her.

▶ I've saved the money, but don't know if I should have a nose job or not.

▶ I've been offered another good job, but I like the one I've got.

▶ I don't know whether to get married this year or next year.

You'll see from these examples that there is a considerable overlap between problem-solving and decision-making. Sometimes you'll need to do one and not the other, but more often you may have to look for solutions to a problem and then decide which one to go for. So bear in mind that you may need to switch from one set of skills to the other.

Mythbuster

Myth: If you're depressed, all you need to do is 'pull yourself together' and 'snap out of it'.

Truth: 'Pulling yourself together', whatever that means, or 'snapping out of it' is what a depressed person is constantly trying to do, making them tense, stressed and anxious. But depression doesn't work that way. To get better, they need to know how, and might need medication as well as sessions of talking treatment.

PROBLEM-SOLVING

Whatever the problem, it pays to think as broadly as possible to find for solutions to it. There are ways of doing this that make it easier, and have the potential to uncover ideas and options that you hadn't thought of. You probably already use at least some of the techniques described below, without being aware of it.

Information-gathering and fact-finding

Nowadays we have the luxury of the internet and this approach is so much easier and requires much less effort than when you had to go to a library or other source of information. There are countless search engines, websites and apps to provide you in seconds with what you need to know. You can type in a few key words or a fuller description of the problem and find a myriad sources of information. The drawback with the internet is the reliability of the information, so be cautious and try to identify reputable websites.

Brainstorming

'Brainstorming' is a useful skill for solutions that need creative thinking rather than more information. Get together as many willing people as you can find, although you can do this on your own. Allow your minds to roam unrestrained, thinking 'outside the circle' or 'out of the box' as well as looking for the more obvious solutions. Keep a note of all the ideas, but don't get side-tracked into deciding whether they are good or bad ones or other criticisms or comments; that will come later. You may even experience the 'light bulb switching on in your head' moment depicted so often in cartoons, when a wonderful idea strikes you out of the blue. Social networking sites like Facebook are great for getting other ideas from your friends too.

This process will often result in an idea that is clearly the best solution. Sometimes, however, you'll find you have several good options and it will be difficult to choose between them. The next section in the chapter explains how to make a decision quickly and without going over and over things.

Quick fix: Simple massage

Place the flat of the first three fingers of each hand on your temples, the soft area at the side of your head just above where your cheekbones end. Apply gentle but firm pressure for 20 seconds (or more if you want to). You can also cup your cheeks in the palms of your hands at the same time.

DECISION-MAKING

The choices involved in a decision will often be self-evident from the start. Apply for this job, or don't apply. Buy the slinky silver dress or the little black number. Go to the party, or don't go. But sometimes the decision is more complicated. The techniques below explain how to make decisions, starting with more straightforward decisions, and moving on to dealing with more complicated or less clear-cut decisions.

Making an informed choice

As with problem-solving, sometimes all you need to make a decision is more information. You can't know everything about everything. So find someone who does or check things out at the library or on the internet. Find out all you can about each option, and think about the possible repercussions. Sometimes the answer is much clearer when you have all the facts, and a good solution may come to light that you hadn't even thought about.

Considering the pros and cons

This is one of the simplest and most widely used techniques for deciding on a course of action. Take a minute to think of a problem you have or a decision you need to make. Then create two columns on a piece of paper; in one column write down all the 'pros' or benefits of a course of action, and in the other column list all the 'cons' or disadvantages associated with it. This should help to clarify things.

You may find that there are an equal number of pros and cons. If this happens, giving a 'weight' or importance to each pro or con will usually help to clarify matters. Go back to your sheet of paper and think about each of the points you have written in the 'Pros' and 'Cons' columns. Assign a score to each point depending how important this factor is in the decision. You could use a scale of 0–10 or 0–100, whatever feels right to you. When you have finished, add up the scores for each column to see whether the pros outweigh the cons or vice versa.

Case study: Meg and her family

Meg is a single mother of three teenage children: Zahra, Louise and Ben. Meg's husband was in the armed forces but was killed in action when the children were small, and she has had mild depression off and on since then. Daughter Zahra usually sails through life, but today has drifted in from school and announced to Meg that she needs her help with something. Meg heads for the sewing box, expecting to have a button to sew back on or a ripped seam to fix. But Zahra blurts out that she can't decide whether or not to take French A-level at school next year. Meg instead gets out paper and a pencil and together she and Zahra weigh up the pros and cons.

Problem: Should I take French A-level next year at school?			
Pros (for)		**Cons (against)**	
I really like French	10	My best friend isn't taking it	5
I like the teacher	6	There's all that vocabulary to learn	5
I want to go on the school trip to France	8	I have a bad memory	3
I've learned a bit of French already	6	People say the verbs are difficult	4
Lessons are very hands-on and practical	8	You have to have an oral exam	6
Lessons are fun	5	It means I can't take Music	6
It would be good for the future	8	There's lots of homework	4
		Angela will be in my class and I can't stand her	2
TOTAL SCORE	51	TOTAL SCORE	35

OTHER PROBLEM-SOLVING AND DECISION-MAKING TIPS

Here are some other helpful tips.

▶ Plan ahead – be aware of what's coming up in your life. Don't leave everything to the last minute, when it's too late to gather information.

▶ Don't rush decisions – take your time, and think things through. It's often worth sleeping on a decision, as your whole perception of the situation can change if you take your mind off it for a while. (Planning ahead gives you the chance to do this.)

- Try before you buy – make the decision but don't act on it for a few days, if time allows. Spend those few days pretending or visualizing that you've made the decision and see how it feels to you.

- Accept that we all make mistakes. Millions of decisions are made every day. And how often do people decide later that it might have been better if they had made a different decision? It's important for us all to learn early what failure and disappointment feel like. This will make us stronger and more resilient people.

Mythbuster

Myth: You should just wait for the depression to get better by itself.

Truth: Depression can be very severe and there's no saying how long it will last. Treating it will make it less severe, it will get better sooner and it will be less likely to come back.

Panic attacks

Many people with depression have sudden attacks of acute anxiety or panic. These can appear from nowhere and then decline and disappear again, lasting anything from several minutes to half an hour. Having experienced attacks myself, I know what terrifying experiences they can be.

Most people have now heard of panic attacks, also called anxiety attacks, but at the time I had my first one they were little known. The nightmare of feelings seemed to come out of the blue, overwhelm me and then go away again just as unpredictably. One minute I was enjoying a lovely sunny day; the next minute I felt as if the world was collapsing around me. It is called an attack and that is what it felt like.

A panic attack is actually more predictable and understandable than it seems. Consequently, it is also easier to deal with. We'll come on to these aspects later, but first, what do you already know about panic attacks?

Your thinking space

❋ Had you heard of a panic or anxiety attack before you read this book?

❋ If you've had a panic attack, how long did it last?

❋ How often have you had a panic attack? What do you do when it happens? Does this help?

❋ Do you notice any other symptoms in your body or mind when you panic?

❋ Do you know anyone who has panic attacks? A relative? A friend?

Not everyone who is depressed will experience panic. And not everyone who has a panic attack is depressed or stressed. Many people have only one panic attack; it never happens again, and there is no associated long-term anxiety problem. But for others, these attacks happen more than once and they can be part of a broader pattern, as mine were. Panic attacks, or a longer lasting general feeling of low-grade panic or fear, can be part of depression. The NHS Choices website estimated in 2012 that one person in ten in Great Britain experienced occasional panic attacks. That's over 5 million people.

The first thing you notice during an attack may be your stomach turning over or churning, or butterflies in your stomach. You may feel your heart begin to race and your breathing become faster. You may feel hot and sweaty, light-headed and overwhelmed by fear and panic. Some people feel an urgent need to escape from wherever they are at the time. This might be at home, the supermarket, the bank or driving on the motorway; I've known people flee from the hairdresser's with their hair half-dried. Some people find themselves rooted to the spot, completely unable to move. However the panic attack affects you, it is a distressing and frightening experience.

Panic attacks are part of the body's 'fight, flight or freeze' reaction, which happens automatically when we are in physical danger to give us the energy and muscle strength to run away from or fight whatever is threatening us. This instinct can also lead some animals to freeze into immobility to avoid attack, and it can have the same effect on people too. Such attacks last a maximum of 20–30 minutes because our bodies can't sustain this emergency reaction for any longer. It a very primitive, but life-saving instinct. If we had to take the time to work out what to do when our child steps off the pavement into a busy road, it could already be too late. The 'fight or flight' reaction impels us to act before we have time to think. Understanding this explains our physical reaction – the racing heart, muscle tension and, for most people, an almost irresistible need to move from where we are to somewhere safer, such as our car or home.

But why do you panic when there's no reason for it? The simple answer is that your brain thinks there is a reason for it. And that might be due to a fleeting thought you've had and didn't even notice, such as:

▶ I'm going to be late again.

▶ What if I can't get this done in time?

▶ What if I can't pay those bills?

▶ What if I panic now?

Questions and thoughts like these are a common source of anxiety, which your brain registers as danger, and can set off the feared panic attack. People who are depressed or anxious often have many 'What if…' questions going round in their heads. The thought, 'What if I panic now?' tends to be self-fulfilling.

Panic attacks can also be triggered by associations: if you go to a place where you've panicked before, or there's a familiar smell or sound which reminds you of a place where you'd had a bad experience. Our sense of smell can make very strong associations, both good and bad. The smell of the dentist's still gives me butterflies, and some people can't go into a hospital without panicking.

A panic attack is the 'fight, flight or freeze' response occurring when a body isn't in any physical danger, and that's why it feels so bad. If you did actually have to run or fight, your body would be geared up for it and your body's response wouldn't feel wrong at all. We don't want to turn off this response – there will be times when you need it. What you need is to know how to cope if you have a panic attack.

Quick fix

If you like music, listen to something that always makes a difference to your mood. Put together some tracks that always lift your mood, and have them nearby for when you need them.

THE PAUSE TECHNIQUE

Because the panic response is an automatic process, like breathing, you'll probably have found that just telling yourself not to panic doesn't work. Physical techniques, on the other hand, bypass the automatic response, allowing the brain to realize that the danger is not real, and press the 'no need to panic' button. The PAUSE technique described below shows you how to do this.

It's easier to avert a panic attack if you catch it at the start. Although an attack may seem to happen so quickly that there is no warning, if you learn to recognize the signs, you can use relaxation or breathing techniques to avoid the attack progressing any further. It's common for an attack to begin with a lurch in the stomach, your heart rate rising or an awareness of muscle tension increasing quickly. But whatever stage the attack reaches, the PAUSE technique will help you to reduce it from the level of a hurricane to a storm, or even a passing shower.

▶ Work out what the first signs of a panic attack. This might be a feeling in your stomach, a thought in your mind, your heart rate rising, etc.

▶ Be on the lookout for those first signs.

When you're gripped by panic, it's hard to think straight. The PAUSE technique is specially designed to be easy to remember in the midst of panic. The letters P...A...U...S...E spell out what to do, and the technique not only stops the panic attack going any further, but also makes it less likely to happen again. For many people it works first time, but for others it can take a bit of practice. If it doesn't work for you the first time, then persevere and it will give you back control over something that seemed uncontrollable.

The PAUSE technique

When you notice your first signs of panic:

1 Pause ... and make yourself comfortable

2 Absorb ... detail of what's going on around you

3 Use ... any method of relaxing quickly that works well for you, then

4 Slowly ... when you feel better

5 Ease ... yourself back into what you were doing.

Next steps

The key points covered in Chapter 7 are:

✳ **what mindfulness is**

✳ **how mindfulness can help with depression**

✳ **techniques to try**

✳ **how mindfulness can help prevent recurrences of depression**

✳ **meditation and depression.**

7

Mindfulness and depression

Mindfulness is one of the simplest techniques for treating depression, and the most effective in relieving anxiety and depression. Mindfulness is an ancient skill that has been practised around the world for centuries to help people feel calmer and more centred. Despite this, it is a relatively new technique for treating depression, introduced only in the past 20 years or so, as research has shown that using mindfulness regularly can produce an improvement for most depressed people.

How do you feel?

1 How would you describe the pace of your average day? (Choose all that apply.)

    a Very slow
    b Don't really have an average day, they're all different
    c Pace varies throughout the day
    d On the go all day, but steady pace
    e Feel as if I'm running all day, just to keep up

2 How many items are on your average daily 'to do' list (either a written list or in your head)?

    a None
    b I don't really think that way
    c Between 1 and 3
    d Between 4 and 7
    e Too many to count

3 If you travel somewhere by car, whether as the driver or passenger, and park in a large car park, how easy is it for you to remember where the car is when you return to it?

    a I always remember
    b Don't really think about it
    c Some days better than others
    d I rely on the driver remembering
    e Really hard to remember

4 How familiar are you with the idea of mindfulness? (Choose any that apply.)

    a Never heard of it
    b Have heard about it, but don't know what it is
    c Have a rough idea what it is, but haven't tried it
    d Have tried it
    e Use it and find it helpful

5 How busy would you say your mind is most of the time? (Choose any that apply.)

    a My mind's never busy.
    b Always busy. I can't get it to stop.
    c So busy I can't think straight.
    d Worst when I have to make a decision.
    e Only busy some times.

What is mindfulness?

Mindfulness isn't an aim or a destination to work towards, it's simply a way of being. This explanation sounds a bit way out but in fact it couldn't be less so. The best way to explain mindfulness for you to feel what it's like for yourself.

As you read this, you are looking at the letters and words and interpreting them, deciding what each word and each sentence means. You're paying attention to commas and full stops, to help you make sense of each sentence. You are doing this without thinking, but now that I've described the process you're more aware of it.

Now think about your breathing. You've been breathing while you were reading – indeed, for all of your life – but how often do you notice it? Pay attention to it now. As you take your next breath in, can you feel your chest or tummy moving? Notice your next inward breath, too. And what can you hear around you? What sounds are reaching your ears? As you've been doing this, you have been mindful. You're in the 'here and now', slowly noticing your body and what your senses are experiencing. That's mindfulness.

Mythbuster

Myth: I can't try mindfulness. It's against my religion.

Truth: Mindfulness has no religious associations at all, so anyone can try it.

A LOST SKILL

Being mindful is a skill we always had but many of us have forgotten in today's hectic existence. It's so easy for your mind to be occupied with thoughts about the day or week ahead and never notice the moment you're actually living in. And that's where our life is lived, in the moment. Being mindful brings your mind from the past or the future into the here and now, into the moment. And you absorb the detail of that moment.

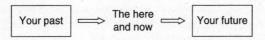

You're mindful as you watch waves quietly lap the shore, listening to the sound and thinking of nothing else. Sitting quietly on a train, listening to the noise of the wheels on the rails and watching the countryside go past is being mindful. Even gazing at the people streaming past you in a city centre as you sit on a bench, observing the movement and listening to the changing sounds without any other distractions, is mindfulness.

How to live more mindfully

Mindfulness is a way of being and a way of life which can provide an escape from the hustle and bustle of everyday life. A talking therapy that includes mindfulness or a mindfulness course will teach you more about it, but here are some ideas about how to create a more mindful lifestyle.

How to be mindful for at least five minutes a day

▶ 'Be' in the here and now, as much as you can. Use any opportunities in your day to do this; while waiting for something or someone is an ideal time. Build up from five minutes a day.

▶ In the shower or bath, smell the fragrances, feel the water and the towel on your skin, hear the sounds only a bath or shower can make, feel your bare feet on the bathroom floor.

▶ At meal times, eat more slowly and be aware of each mouthful of food. Notice how the food is presented, the textures, flavours, the aroma.

▶ Wherever you go, notice people and their expressions, clothing, hair. Soak up colour and texture, really listen to the sounds of people going about their business. Notice the weather around you – a breeze, sunshine, a shower. Don't miss those interesting smells as you pass the coffee shop or the perfume counter.

▶ When walking somewhere, do it mindfully and just be in the moment. Be aware of your toes and feet in your shoes, the sensations in your muscles, the sound and the feeling as you put your weight on each foot in turn. Are you cold or warm? Take in everything around you – noises, smells, colours, people.

Quick fix

When you're ready, close your eyes and imagine that you've been blind from birth, so you have no idea what colour is. Imagine that all you've had to go on is what people have said about colour. Spend 2–3 minutes with your eyes closed thinking about this. Then slowly open your eyes as if you're seeing the world and all its variety of colour and shape for the first time. Enjoy it as if you'd never seen it before. That's how we should enjoy our world every day.

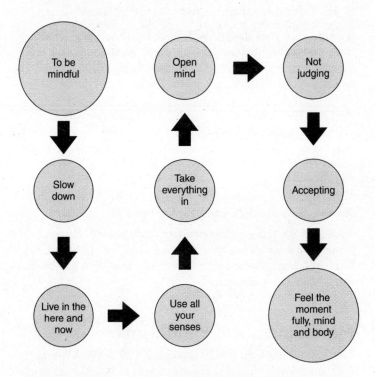

The benefits of mindfulness

When I learned mindfulness, I found it incredibly helpful. It was a 'light bulb' moment for me, as it did two things:

▶ It showed me instantly that I had been spending too much time with my head in the past or in the future, but seldom in the here and now. I was always thinking back to everything that happened yesterday, or ahead to what I had to get done today and how I was going to do it.

▷ It showed me that the phrase 'get into the here and now' was easy to follow, like a signpost. I found that with little effort I could be in the here and now, feeling as if I'd come to a sudden halt and able to see clearly around myself for the first time in months. I could almost hear my nervous system crying out 'Thank you, thank you' because I had at last taken my foot off the accelerator pedal, and my mind was no longer filled with stress about the past or worry about the future.

'Mindfulness' provides you with these benefits, taking 'here and now' thinking further by showing you more ways to come into the moment, and more ways to make maximum use of this. I touched on mindfulness in Chapter 6 when I introduced the PAUSE technique for dealing with panic attacks. Can you see the link? The 'A' in PAUSE stands for 'Absorb detail around you'; in other words, be mindful.

Mythbuster

Myth: Mindfulness encourages slowing down and being in the moment. This takes away your spark, your oomph, and your drive to succeed.

Truth: Quite the opposite. Mindfulness rests the mind and calms your thinking, but doesn't stop it altogether. So it makes it easier to plan, make decisions, find solutions and come up with new ideas. And it gives more energy to your spark and oomph!

Mindfulness and Buddhism

Mindfulness has been closely connected with the Buddhist faith for thousands of years, but it can be used easily and successfully quite separately from any religious links. It is just a means of clearing your mind and concentrating on the here and now that many belief systems have used for centuries. Any type of 'prayer' encourages this experience. Meditation, which you could call mindfulness's big brother, has very similar roots, but it has not been studied in such depth in connection with depression. It is, however, another skill that works well even when detached from a belief system, and will produce a state of very deep relaxation, although this takes more skill and practice to achieve. There is more about meditation in Chapter 10.

Quick fix

If your mood looks up a little, even for an instant, revel in that moment and thoroughly enjoy it. Remember what it feels like so that it will be easier to do it again.

Mythbuster

Myth: Restless or agitated people with poor concentration can't expect to be able to be quiet and focus in a mindful way.

Truth: Most people, even those with poor concentration, learn this new skill gradually. So everyone can do it, and the restless and agitated among us will probably gain more than most.

Mindfulness and depression

The use of mindfulness as therapy was first studied by Dr Jon Kabat-Zinn, emeritus professor of medicine at the University of Massachusetts, who began his work on the subject over 30 years ago. NICE now recommends mindfulness-based stress reduction programmes for stress. Mindfulness also forms the basis of mindfulness-based cognitive therapy (MBCT); a 2000 study at Oxford University found that the relapse rate for those who had three or more previous episodes of depression was improved by taking a class in MBCT over an eight-week period. Mindfulness plays a part in making us more resilient to both stress and depression too (see Chapters 11 and 15).

Case study: Nathan

Nathan, age 41, has a partner and a four-year-old son. He is a project manager and enjoyed his work until about six months ago, when his role was changed and he had to do much more travelling. He really missed his family and friends when he was away, and the stress and tension when he was on work trips was becoming hard to bear. He started to worry that he would have a recurrence of the depression he'd had five years before. Browsing through a magazine at the dentist's one day, he came across an article on mindful walking and decided to give it a try in the evenings the next time he was away from home. He found it easy to do, and he felt much better after having a mindful walk each evening after work. He still misses his family, but he phones home after his walk and enjoys a chat without all the tension he was experiencing. He even came up the idea of using his laptop so that they could see each other too, and he could read his son a bedtime story.

 Next steps

The key points covered in Chapter 8 are:
✴ **ways to get your message across better**
✴ **how to set useful goals**
✴ **ways to have more control of your mood**
✴ **what neuro-linguistic programming (NLP) is**
✴ **more ways to cope better with depression.**

8

NLP and depression

Neuro-linguistic programming (NLP) sounds like a complex psychological subject, but the abbreviation of the name, NLP, may more familiar. NLP is essentially a box of powerful tools for you to use, bringing together much that is of practical use for everyone. This chapter will pick out for you some of the aspects of NLP that can be particularly useful in overcoming depression.

How do you feel?

1 How familiar are you with the concept of NLP? (Choose any that apply.)

    a Never heard of it.
    b Have heard about it, but don't know what it is.
    c Have a rough idea what it is, but haven't tried it.
    d Have tried it.
    e Use it and find it helpful.

2 When were you happiest in your life?

3 What was it about that time that made you happy?

4 Whenever I smell home-baking, it reminds me of happy days as a child at my grandmother's during summer holidays. What smells or perfumes remind you of a happy time, or just make you feel good?

5 Listening to the songs of pop singer Adele makes me feel thoughtful. What type of music makes you feel:

    a Energetic
    b Sad
    c Happy.

NLP's four rules for success

NLP is about the human mind and thinking. It explores our habits and patterns of thought, and how these play a part in making us behave as we do. It sets out to improve these thought processes so that they work better for us and improve everything we do. This includes providing tools that we can use to make us feel better if we are depressed.

A fundamental part of NLP is its Four Rules for Success. These are profound rules that apply no matter what you're doing.

1 Use all five senses to be fully aware of what's happening around you.

2 Be flexible – be open to new thoughts and other ways of doing things.

3   Take time to work out what you want from your life.

4   Be ready to take action and make changes to achieve what you want from life.

Although NLP takes under its umbrella many different ideas and practical uses, at its centre there is a set of founding beliefs and assumptions. These link all aspects of NLP together, and can have far-reaching implications for how we choose to lead our lives.

Here are four of NLP's underlying beliefs. They are particularly helpful to think about if you are feeling anxious or depressed, as they can ease a troubled mind or calm disturbing thoughts. Take a few minutes to think about each of these statements and assess how relevant it might be to you and your life.

▶ If what you're doing isn't working, do something different.

▶ Everyone sees the world through different eyes.

▶ Behind every action there is a positive intention.

▶ We can all change our beliefs, goals and motivations if we want to.

Anchoring your thoughts

When you're angry, down or sad, do you find that playing loud or upbeat music helps you deal with that unwanted energy and emotion? Or does listening to music you enjoy work better for you? Sounds, music and all sorts of sensations can affect us deeply, especially those that already have associations for us. Retailers know this, and use research to decide what type of music to play in different areas of their shops in order to encourage us to choose particular items, to linger longer in the shop, or to buy or eat more.

For many people, the sounds or music that are the most relaxing are not necessarily quiet and peaceful. This is because your mood can also depend on the associations the sounds or music have for you. For instance, Christmas sounds and music, like sleigh bells, 'White Christmas', or Noddy Holder from Slade shouting 'It's Christmas!' instantly make many people feel whatever feelings they associate with Christmas. For some, the feelings are happy, but for others they may evoke sadness or anxiety. In the same way, the sounds and music we find relaxing are those we associate with previous relaxing experiences. Deliberately using these associations to make ourselves feel more positive or more relaxed and content is called 'anchoring' in NLP.

So if we want to feel happy, then the music from our happy times is likely to help us. The music that helps us to cheer up or unwind is personal to us, and derives from the associations each of us builds up over a lifetime.

'Music is the soundtrack to your life.'
Dick Clark, American radio and TV personality

Quite apart from these personal associations, some music can affect people physically, slowing the heart rate, encouraging relaxed brainwaves, or producing the feel-good endorphins in the brain. The following types of music or particular pieces, all readily available, are effective in producing a relaxed state for most people:

- Bach's 'Air on a G String'
- Chopin's 'Nocturne in G'
- Beethoven's Symphony No. 6 ('The Pastoral')
- Handel's *Water Music*
- Gregorian chants
- Pan pipe music
- Baroque music, e.g. Mozart, Handel, Bach, Vivaldi etc
- Any music whose tempo (like Baroque music) coincides with the average resting heart rate of 60 beats a minute.

Many sounds other than music can also create a calm state. Birdsong, a babbling brook or the slow tick of a clock are typical examples. Some sounds are more relaxing than others, and what works for you is a matter of associations and personal preference. Some people find the sound of so-called 'white noise' very peaceful; this is a mix of all the frequencies of sound, and is similar to the shower running, or the noise from a fan or rain on the roof. It can help you to sleep (and young babies too) and to cope with noisy neighbours, street noise or tinnitus. CDs and downloads of relaxing sounds are now available for every sound imaginable, including websites that broadcast white noise free all day (contact details in Appendix 4).

Mythbuster

Myth: My mother had depression so I'm bound to get it.

Truth: This does increase your chances of having depression a little, but it doesn't mean you will definitely get depression. And at least you can learn all about it so you'll know what to do if it does happen.

Anchoring with guided imagery

In guided imagery, you use your own imagination to bring to mind the images and sounds that can act as your anchor for your thoughts. It may take a little practice at first, but you can build up gradually once you have the idea.

This is the process to follow.

▶ Choose one of the two scenarios described below, and read the description. You can make a recording of the description if that is easier.

▶ When you're happy that you know what to do, lie down or sit somewhere warm and comfortable, and relax your body using any technique that works for you.

▶ Then close your eyes slowly and imagine yourself in your chosen setting. Imagine as much detail as you can, using all your senses: hear, see, feel, smell.

▶ Take as long as you like, but when you want to stop, slowly let go of your image and become more and more aware of your surroundings, until you are fully alert again.

Scenario 1: A summer stream

You're warm and comfortable, lying or sitting by a gurgling stream ... it's warm and sunny in the countryside ... the birds are singing in the trees ... leaves are fluttering in the warm breeze ... the air is clean and fresh ... you can feel the warmth of the sunshine on your skin...

Scenario 2: Your favourite place

You're safe and warm in your own special comfortable place ... you choose where it is ... anywhere you feel happy and relaxed ... where are you? ... see it clearly ... what do you hear? ... what sensations can you feel? ... what are you doing?...

 Quick fix

Spray the room with a fragrance you really like. Keep a selection of favourites by you. Anything will do: air fresheners, perfumes, fruit sprays such as orange or spicy sprays like cinnamon. It works in the car and at the office too.

How to audit your life

You can 'audit' your life, to see the bigger picture and identify the healthy and the problem areas, in just the same way as you can audit your financial situation. A 'life audit' explores all aspects of your life. You'll need between 30 minutes to an hour to do this.

▶ Place these ten headings, equally spaced, down the left-hand side of a blank page in your personal journal:

▷ where you live

▷ your family

▷ personal relationships

▷ friends and social life

▷ work or career

▷ money

▷ your health

▷ fun and recreation

▷ inner soul and spirit

▷ personal growth and learning.

▶ Without thinking too deeply about it, give each of these headings a score out of ten to show how happy you are with it (10 being the top mark). Note your score next to the heading.

▶ When you have scored all ten headings, look over your scores.

▷ How do these make you feel?

▷ Which are the highest? Why?

▷ Which are the lowest? Why?

▶ Choose the area of your life that you would want to improve first. This might be the one with the lowest score, but it might not be.

▶ Thinking about this part of your life, consider:

▷ what is making you unhappy with it?

▷ how would you go about making improvements? Jot these ideas down.

▷ if you need more thinking time, come back to this later.

Knowing where you're going

It helps to know where you're going. Having even a few clear goals gives life purpose, structure and meaning. As Benjamin Franklin, one of the founding fathers of the USA, said: 'If you fail to plan, you plan to fail.'

Although it's true that there is no failure, only feedback, your chances of success will increase the clearer and more thought-out your goals are. Having clear goals and knowing how and when you expect to reach them can help to lower your stress level. It can also boost your self-esteem and your feeling of having control of your life. NLP tends not to use terms like 'goal' or 'objective', however, preferring to use the term 'desirable outcome' instead.

A desirable outcome should:

▶ be positive: 'I want…', rather than 'I don't want…'

▶ be clearly within your control

▶ be clear and specific

▶ be within your ability (skills and resources)

▶ not produce negative outcomes as a by-product

▶ have a clear first step.

Examples of well-formed desirable outcomes would be:

▶ I want to have a chicken salad sandwich for lunch today, and I'm going to make it now.

▶ I want to learn how to play the acoustic guitar, and I'm dropping in at the music college on Friday to find out about their lessons.

There is no failure

The statement 'There is no failure, only feedback' is one of the most well-known in NLP. It makes the point that there's no need to feel bad when we feel we've failed; we tried, and that's what matters. As Oscar Wilde put it, 'Experience is the name every one gives to their mistakes'. The American composer John Powell said, 'The only real mistake is the one from which we learn nothing.'

Life moves quickly, and we are constantly adjusting and adapting to what it brings. Priorities change. Needs change. And sometimes we make what turns out to be a mistake. What NLP tells us is that we don't need to beat ourselves up about making a mistake because we haven't. There are no mistakes and no failure, only feedback. And this feedback is crucial for us to reassess where we are in our lives and make any necessary changes so we are ready to move forward again.

Next steps
The key points covered in Chapter 9 are:
* **the role of medication in treating depression**
* **the various types of medication, and what they do**
* **how long medication is needed**
* **the pros and cons of medication**
* **whether herbal remedies can be effective.**

9

Medication for depression

When depression is mentioned, many people immediately think about pills. Although there are many other approaches and therapies, medication remains one of the most commonly used and most effective ways of relieving the symptoms of moderate to severe depression, either on its own or alongside other forms of treatment. It is very common to have anxiety along with depression, and mixed anxiety and depression is the most common mental health problem in Britain today. Fortunately, this combination responds well to medication for most people.

There are almost 30 different kinds of antidepressant available today. These fall into several distinct types, each of which works in a different way. Understanding more about the way different medications work will help you to make informed choices about treatment, and so be more successful on your journey towards recovery.

How do you feel?

1 What is your general feeling about taking medication for depression? (Choose all that apply.)

  a If it's going to help, there's no problem.
  b I'd really hate having to take it.
  c I wouldn't take it.
  d I'd feel I'd failed somehow.

2 If you or someone you know has taken prescribed medication for depression, how helpful has this been overall?

  a Not sure
  b A success
  c Helped somewhat
  d No help at all

3 Have you or anyone you know experienced any side-effects of antidepressants?

  a Yes
  b No

If you answered 'Yes', what the side-effects like?

4 Have you ever used a herbal remedy for depression (e.g. St John's wort)?

  a Yes
  b No

If you answered 'Yes', how useful was this?

5 Have you or anyone you know ever stopped taking antidepressants?

  a Yes
  b No

If you answered 'Yes', what was this like?

Prescribed medication

If you are diagnosed with depression, medication is one of a number of options that your doctor will consider in deciding how best to meet your needs. Prescribed medication definitely has a place in the treatment of moderate to severe depression, although it is unlikely to be prescribed for mild depression unless this has been resistant to other treatments (see Chapter 4). More effective drugs have been developed in the past few decades, so even if you've tried medication before without benefiting from it, it's worth considering again.

There are a number of different types of antidepressant, and many different medications within each type, so one medication out of the range will be the right one for you. With so many different drugs available, this chapter can only cover the broader categories but this should give you the basic knowledge and understanding you need if you have to take decisions about medication. Further information about the different drugs is available online (see also Appendix 4) or from your doctor.

Point to remember

If you have any questions about taking medication for depression, your doctor is the best person to speak to. If you're already taking medication, don't make any changes without talking to your doctor first. Bear in mind that doctors don't have the time to explain everything to all their patients, so they work on an 'explain if the patient asks' basis. So never be afraid to ask. Don't leave the surgery regretting what you didn't find out.

Myth	Truth
If I get depressed, all I need to do is take an antidepressant and I'll be OK.	You won't begin to feel the benefit of antidepressant medication for two to three weeks, and it won't achieve its maximum effect for at least six weeks, maybe more.
All antidepressants are the same. It doesn't matter which one you take.	Antidepressants are all different, and it can take time to find the right one for you.
Pills can't really help a 'mental' problem.	Depression affects mood and emotions, but it also has physical symptoms. Medication works on the physical symptoms, and also on the brain chemistry which causes both the physical and mental symptoms of depression.
Pills are just a crutch. They don't get to the root of the problem.	Antidepressants can't sort out personal or financial problems, but they can relieve your depression enough for you to do something about these for yourself. Sometimes, the medication is all that's needed to make you feel better.

(Continued)

Myth	Truth
Antidepressants are addictive.	Antidepressants are not addictive, in the sense that your body will crave the drug if you stop taking it suddenly. However, you should wean yourself off antidepressants gradually, just as you would with other medications, to avoid withdrawal effects while your body adjusts. Your doctor will advise you about this when the time comes.
I'll never get off the antidepressants.	When you are well again, and the doctor feels it's time, you'll be weaned off the antidepressants. A small number of people who have had several relapses may be considered for longer-term use – but if this keeps them free of depression, that's a real benefit. Many people have conditions that need medication for life (e.g. diabetics, transplant patients, those with high blood pressure or heart disease), but this keeps them fit and well, so we don't question it. Mental health problems are no different.
As soon as I feel better, I can stop taking my pills.	Antidepressants are a bit like antibiotics. You must complete the course, even if you're feeling better. Wait till the doctor thinks it's time. At the earliest, this is likely to be six months after the last symptom has gone.
Antidepressants are just 'happy pills' that cover up how I really feel.	The media applied the term 'happy pills' for antidepressants, but this is misleading. Antidepressants aim to take away bad, negative feelings and bring you back to your normal self. They don't make you 'happy' as such (see Chapter 14). Antidepressants work on your brain chemistry, changing it slightly in ways which make you feel more like your old self.
Antidepressants just don't work for some people.	The first antidepressant you try may not be the right one for you, and so it may not work; this is common. Or this belief may relate to treatment some years ago, when antidepressants were less effective. But there are many new antidepressants, so if this happens, go back to your doctor and discuss it.
Antidepressants have unpleasant side-effects.	All medications have side-effects, but newer antidepressants have fewer and they are milder. The side-effects can also wear off as you adjust to the medication or they can be lessened in other ways. Talk to your doctor or pharmacist about this. Don't be put off by the leaflet with the medication that lists side-effects – these lists have to include every known side-effect, however unusual, for legal reasons and for complete transparency.

Myths about medication for depression

THE DEVELOPMENT OF ANTIDEPRESSANTS

The development of drugs to combat depression began in the 1950s, and arose largely by chance when it was noticed that drugs for other conditions reduced symptoms of depression. An example of this was a drug used to treat tuberculosis which was also found to improve the patient's mood. The outcome of early research was the development of drugs which worked on the chemical messengers in the brain, especially serotonin and noradrenaline, to lift your mood. This is still the main function of antidepressants to this day.

Out of this early research, two types of antidepressants were created. These were the tricyclics, such as Anafranil and Tryptizol, and the monoamine oxidase inhibitors (MAOIs), such as Nardil. These two types are the least often prescribed today. Developments since then have focused on making antidepressants more efficient and reducing the side-effects. Three other main types have been developed since 1987:

- SSRIs (selective serotonin re-uptake inhibitors)
- SNRIs (serotonin and noradrenaline re-uptake inhibitors)
- NASSAs (noradrenaline and specific serotoninergic antidepressants).

SSRIs

Most people have heard of a drug called Prozac, one of the first antidepressants to be developed in the class of drugs known as selective serotonin re-uptake inhibitors (SSRIs). These drugs alter the way the brain chemistry works, so that the brain re-absorbs less serotonin, increasing the amount remaining to work in your brain. It was soon realized that many of these drugs also reduce anxiety, so SSRIs are also commonly prescribed for mixed anxiety and depression.

Examples (brand name in brackets) include:

- Fluoxetene (Prozac), first approved for use in the USA in 1987
- Paroxetene (Seroxat), first approved for use in the USA in 1992.

SNRIs

As its name suggests, this type of antidepressant not only discourages the brain from re-absorbing serotonin, it also discourages the re-uptake of another chemical messenger, noradrenaline. An example is:

▶ Venlafaxine (Efexor)

NASSAs

In the case of this type of antidepressant, alpha-2 receptors in the brain are blocked by the medication. This enhances the action of both of the important chemical messengers, serotonin and noradrenaline. An example is:

▶ Mirtazapine (Zispin)

Point to remember

The NICE guidance on depression in 2012 suggests that mild depression may get better without treatment, and that in less severe cases talking therapies such as CBT, and exercise, especially outdoors, may be more helpful than antidepressants.

Taking antidepressants

Often we open new medication and just take the tablet, ignoring the leaflet inside the box. But it's important with any medication, and especially medication for depression, to take the time to read this leaflet. If your concentration isn't good, ask a friend or family member to read it for you, or ask the pharmacist to talk it over with you. The patient information leaflet (PIL) is packed with useful information, including:

▶ what conditions the drug is licensed to treat

▶ if the drug may slow you down generally, or make you sleepier than usual

▶ anything you should be aware of before taking the drug, such as medical conditions which mean you shouldn't take it

▶ whether you can take it if you're pregnant or breastfeeding

- what time of day to take it, and whether before or after food
- whether alcohol or any particular foods should be avoided
- whether your driving might be affected
- how long it will be until you feel the drug begin to work
- how long the drug will take to achieve its maximum effect
- what to do if you forget a dose
- possible side-effects
- a full list of ingredients, including materials used to make the tablet or capsule
- how to store the drug safely.

All of this is important information because:

- taking your medication in the correct way is essential for you to gain the most benefit from it
- it's easy to forget a dose when you're tired and have poor concentration or a poor memory because you're depressed
- knowing about possible side-effects in advance prevents anxiety if you do experience them, as does knowing that most side-effects wear off as your body adjusts. But note that although there may be a long list of possible side-effects, most of these are highly unlikely to occur; those listed as affecting one in ten people are the most likely, but nine out of ten people won't have these either.
- the ingredients may contain an item you're allergic to
- you will not think the medication is not working if you are aware that most antidepressants take several weeks to start to have an effect and even longer to achieve their maximum effect.

An understanding of the medication you are taking will improve your confidence in the treatment and reduce any anxieties you may have. This in turn will improve how effective the medication will be.

Case study: Paulina Porizkova

The former supermodel Paulina Porizkova was born in Czechoslovakia in 1965. When her parents fled the country, Paulina was left in the care of her grandmother. The family was reunited after seven years, but not for long, as Paulina's parents divorced. Her modelling career took off after she appeared on the cover of the *Sports Illustrated* swimsuit issue in 1984, aged just 18. During her career, she appeared in numerous magazines and for a time was the face of Estée Lauder cosmetics. In 2007, she took part in ABC TV's *Dancing with the Stars*, and her worst nightmare happened: she was the first to be voted off. The feeling of rejection caused by this very public vote caused her to develop panic attacks and depression. These problems stayed with her until she sought help and was treated successfully with antidepressants.

DON'T GIVE UP

Taking your medication in the right way, being aware of possible side-effects and the time it should take to have an effect on your symptons will all help you to recognize if you're not feeling better when you should be. If the medication doesn't not seem to be working, you should see your doctor again. Most doctors will monitor your progress anyway, so you'll probably have a regular chance to ask any questions. But whether or not this is the case, see your doctor if you're not improving as the PIL says you should be.

It is quite common for the first type of medication you take not to have any effect. People often have to try a second or even a third type of medication before finding the one that works for them, so don't give up on all medication just because the first prescription doesn't work. Although depression can make you react strongly to a disappointment, it's worth persisting until you find the medication best suited to you.

COMING OFF MEDICATION

Studies show that you are less likely to become depressed again if you stay on your antidepressant medication for at least six months after full recovery. The British National Formulary, which provides expert advice on the use of medicines, recommends that people should keep taking the effective dose for at least six months (or about 12 months in older people) after the depression has lifted. If you stop the treatment too soon, the depression is more likely to come back. If you have recurrent depression, you may need to take an effective, or 'maintenance', dose of your antidepressants for several years. Information about maintenance doses is included in each drug's PIL.

Some studies suggest that most people aren't being given sufficient antidepressants for long enough. If you've had two or more moderate or severe episodes of depression previously, NICE recommends staying on medication for at least two years after you feel well again. Your doctor may also offer other long-term support, so make sure to keep in touch with them.

When you start to come off the medication, you should cut down gradually, with a doctor's guidance, over a period of a month at the very least.

Each drug has a different set of effects that you may experience when you reduce the dosage. These are called 'discontinuation effects', and you'll probably find these explained in the PIL. Discontinuation effects can last for up to a week, and are usually mild but occasionally can be severe. The discontinuation effects that most antidepressants have in common are:

► restlessness

► unsteadiness

► mood changes

► difficulty sleeping

► altered sensations

► sweating

► abdominal symptoms.

If you have severe effects when you are reducing your medication, see your doctor, who will probably slow down your reduction rate or swap you onto another drug that tends to have less of these effects. Some drugs, such as Paroxetine

(Seroxat), leave the body faster than others, and they should be reduced more gradually than, say, Fluoxetine, which is lost much more slowly.

Mythbuster

Myth: If it's natural, it must be safe.

Truth: Of course many natural products are safe, but some are harmful, and some are deadly. Yet, in a 2008 Mori poll, 40 per cent of those polled said they believed that if something was natural, it was safe. The dosage is important too. Warfarin is used in small amounts to prevent blood from clotting, but has been used in larger amounts as a poison for rats and other small animals. You also have to be careful about the combination of different drugs; some drugs found in health food shops may be safe on their own but can have a powerful effect on other conditions you have or medications you might be taking. For instance, garlic and Ginkgo biloba can cause bleeding if you are taking warfarin, while ginseng can increase blood pressure.

St John's wort (Hypericum)

Since 2011, all herbal medicines have been required to have a product licence or to be registered. These measures, however, come nowhere near the depth of research and testing required for the medicines your doctor prescribes.

St John's wort, also called Hypericum, is a herbal antidepressant that you can buy, without a prescription, from pharmacies. It has became a popular over-the-counter treatment for depression. However, in 2012 the NICE guidelines about the use of St John's wort were changed.

'Although there is evidence that St John's wort may be of benefit in mild or moderate depression, practitioners should not prescribe or advise its use by people with depression because of uncertainty about appropriate doses, persistence of effect, variation in the nature of preparations and potential serious interactions with other drugs (including oral contraceptives, anticoagulants and anticonvulsants).'

NICE, 2012

Point to remember

St John's wort should not be used by women who are pregnant or breastfeeding.

Next steps

The key points covered in Chapter 10 are:

✳ **how alternative and complementary treatments can help depression**
✳ **ways of relaxing the mind and body**
✳ **different techniques for you to try**
✳ **self-help and how to find more information or a qualified therapist**
✳ **aromatherapy massage, reflexology, acupuncture, reiki and yoga.**

10

Alternative and complementary treatments

This chapter looks at what alternative and complementary therapies have to offer in relieving depression. The main benefit of these therapies is in relaxing the mind and body, relieving anxiety and enhancing the overall sense of well-being, rather than in treating the depression directly. There are hundreds of alternative and complementary treatments available, but only a selection can be covered here. These are some of the therapies that NICE currently recommends, or the therapies that I consider to be most effective in creating calm in the body and mind. Sometimes, simply feeling pampered and valued can work wonders when you feel down. Also included here are therapies or activities that you can do yourself or that are widely available at a reasonable cost from a qualified therapist, trainer or tutor.

How do you feel?

1 Which alternative and complementary treatments, if any, have you tried?

2 If you have tried some of these treatments, which were moderately or very helpful?

3 If you have tried some of these treatments, were there any which had no effect at all?

4 If you haven't tried any of these treatments, why not?

5 Whether or not you've tried an alternative and complementary treatment, would you prefer one that you can do for yourself, or would you rather have a therapist?

Choosing a therapist, trainer or tutor

If you try out any alternative and complementary treatments, whether they are the therapies or activities mentioned here or other types, it's very important to make sure the therapist, trainer or tutor is fully qualified in their particular field and guidelines for this are listed below. If you don't feel up to looking into this yourself, ask a supportive friend or family member to help you find the right person, and perhaps even go along with you to the first few sessions.

▷ Make sure you know exactly what service is provided, and don't be afraid to ask what will be involved, how many sessions are needed, and at what cost.

▷ Don't be afraid to ask about the practitioner's public liability insurance if the treatment involves physical activity or hands-on treatment, such as yoga or acupuncture.

▷ Classes advertised by reputable organizations, such as a school, college, local authority or adult education association, are usually run by well-qualified and experienced practitioners with adequate insurance.

▷ Reputable organizations, including health spas or complementary therapy centres, usually employ well-qualified staff for the treatments they offer.

- Get a recommendation from someone you know who has been successfully helped with depression.

- Ask for details of at least one satisfied client who has agreed to have a chat with you.

- Only agree to treatment from a therapist:

  ▷ who offers treatments similar to those mentioned in this book

  ▷ who has appropriate insurance

  ▷ whose qualifications are accredited by a recognized authority.

- If you decide to try an alternative or complementary therapy, let your doctor know before you start the therapy, as some should not be undertaken at the same time as other treatment you may be receiving.

> 'Many people find complementary and alternative treatments helpful... When using these therapies and techniques, it is important to work with a qualified and experienced practitioner who is able to offer support appropriate for mental health issues.'
>
> NICE, 2012

Massage

Therapy using massage is said to have originated thousands of years ago in China, and is very relaxing for most people. Several types of healthcare professionals, such as physiotherapists, occupational therapists or massage therapists, can provide massage, as can a range of alternative therapists. That said, a hand massage, or a back or neck rub from a friend or your partner has the same effect.

There are many versions of massage, including shiatsu, aromatherapy massage, Swedish massage, hot stone, Indian head massage, chair massage. These may be available at health spas and complementary health centres, or at a therapist's own practice. Shoulder and neck massages are now on offer in many airport departure lounges and shopping malls. Some employers provide shoulder and neck massage in the workplace as an aid to relieving tension and stress. In some workplaces, you can call for a massage at your desk when you need it. Facials, manicures and pedicures usually include a soothing massage of the area as part of the treatment.

The form of massage you choose depends largely on personal preference, local availability and cost, especially if your budget is limited. A half-hour session can cost from £10 to over £50; a full body massage would usually take an hour.

Reflexology

The origins of reflexology can be traced back to China and India in the third millennium BC. Reflexology is similar to massage, and can sometimes include a foot massage. Specific techniques are used to apply pressure with the hands and fingers to specific areas of the feet, usually without the use of oil or lotion. Reflexology has a range of specific medical purposes, but if you're depressed and you enjoy someone working with your feet, the main effect is to soothe tense feet and encourage bodily relaxation. It has become a very popular alternative therapy in recent years.

Acupuncture

Acupuncture works by inserting very fine needles into parts of the body called acupuncture points. The needles are carefully and painlessly inserted into the acupuncture points, which can be calming and relaxing. Acupuncture has a quick and lasting effect; although the reasons for this are not known at present, it is believed that acupuncture brings about a decrease in the fast delta brainwaves and an increase in the slower alpha brainwaves that are associated with relaxation. Research also shows that acupuncture can lessen both the frequency and severity of tension headaches and migraines, and there is evidence of a calming effect too.

Acupuncture is thought to have originated 5,000 years ago in China, where its effectiveness is ascribed to the energy force running through the body, known as Qi (pronounced 'chee'), travelling throughout the body along pathways known as 'meridians'. The acupuncture points are where the meridians come to the surface of the skin.

Acupressure

Acupressure is an alternative to acupuncture that doesn't use needles. It works by stimulating the same points as in acupuncture, but with pressure from the fingers instead of needles. You can see a therapist for acupressure or, with a little know-how, you can use acupressure on yourself.

Quick fix: Using acupressure on yourself

Make yourself comfortable, either sitting or lying down.

Choose one of the following points:

* The Third Eye: a point located between the eyebrows, in the indentation where the bridge of the nose meets the forehead
* The Heavenly Pillar: a point on the back of the neck slightly below the base of the skull, about half an inch to the left or right of the spine.

Using the flat of one or two fingers, apply firm, steady pressure to your chosen point for two to three minutes. The pressure may cause a mild achy sensation, but should not cause pain.

If you wish to, you can now repeat this process for the other point.

Tai Chi

Tai Chi (pronounced 'tie chee') is a centuries-old martial art that originated in China and has been adopted as a non-competitive exercise regime in the west in recent years. There is a wide variety in the exercise classes that are available, but generally they all aim to achieve harmony with nature and a balance of mental serenity and physical strength, meaning that Tai Chi calms the mind and body while improving physical capability.

Tai Chi consists of detailed sets of choreographed movements and poses, which you work through on your own. Each set is different and can be made up from less than 20 to over 100 separate movements, performed very slowly in a smooth, predetermined sequence while using abdominal breathing. Each sequence is performed with minimum tension in the muscles, and with the mind focused on each step and on remembering the correct order. It is thought that the unhurried, rhythmic movements of the body has the effect of calming the mind and nervous system. The focusing of the mind is very similar to mindfulness (see Chapter 7) and has the same calming effect on your thinking.

Tai Chi is not intended to be strenuous or muscle-building, but to gently exercise the body, calm the mind and stimulate the internal organs. It has grown steadily in popularity, and because little exertion is involved it is suitable for most ages and fitness levels. Most people find that attending a class with a teacher makes the exercises more enjoyable and easier to learn than working by themselves.

Yoga

The word 'yoga' means 'union' in Sanskrit, the language of ancient India, where yoga originated. The name relates to the union between the mind, body and spirit that yoga can bring. What is commonly referred to as yoga in the west can be more accurately described by the Sanskrit word 'asana', or 'hatha', which refers to the aspect of yoga involving the practice of physical postures or poses completed one after the other. This style of yoga promotes total relaxation of the body and mind through concentrating on the specific movements and poses, such as the Lion or the Cat. Other styles of yoga include Vinyasa yoga, and Power yoga, which link poses together and are more physically demanding.

You can easily try hatha yoga at home using a DVD or a book, or at a class locally. Most classes include breathing exercises or a short basic meditation, and often finish with a peaceful session of total relaxation lasting 20 minutes or more. I went regularly to a yoga class when my children were small and found it amazingly helpful for stress and depression. The long relaxation session at the end was particularly re-energizing, and was my first introduction to total body relaxation and the welcome escape from tension it provides. The benefits led me to start having a yoga session every morning at home, and I discovered that the relaxing effect was even greater if I played relaxing music at the same time.

Mythbuster

Myth: You have to be involved in some sort of religion to do yoga.

Truth: Though there is a 'philosophy' or set of ideas attached to the general subject of yoga, the majority of local yoga classes are purely about physical movements and postures and are free of any reference to belief systems.

YOGA BREATHING

Yoga recognizes the importance for our general health and well-being of how we breathe (see also Chapter 6). Yoga breathing, called 'pranayama' in Sanskrit, can be done with the yoga poses or separately, while sitting quietly. Alternate nostril breathing is a well-known yoga breathing exercise, and it is relaxing and calming while also maintaining alertness. There are reports that headaches and blocked sinuses benefit from it too.

Quick fix: Alternate nostril breathing

1. Find somewhere comfortable, and sit in an upright position.
2. Using your right hand, bring your thumb to the right side of your nose and your index finger to the left side.
3. Now gently close off your right nostril with your thumb.
4. Inhale through your left nostril, in your own time.
5. Now close off your left nostril with your index finger, allowing your right nostril to open again.
6. Exhale through your right nostril, in your own time.
7. Inhale through your right nostril.
8. Close off your right nostril with your thumb, allowing your left nostril to open.
9. Exhale through your left nostril.
10. Inhale through your left nostril.
11. Repeat the cycle five to ten times

Meditation

Meditation, which was touched on in Chapter 7, is a simple process similar to mindfulness. Although it has been part of religious practices all over the world in various different forms for thousands of years, its practice doesn't have to be associated with religion or a spiritual belief system.

Meditative techniques are straightforward procedures which can produce deep physical relaxation and a very restful state of mind. An American professor, Patricia Carrington, has reviewed the research on meditation, concluding that meditation produces physiological relaxation similar to deep sleep.

Mythbuster

Myth: You have to sit cross-legged on the floor to meditate.

Truth: You don't have to sit with legs crossed, wear anything special or be a member of a particular religious group to meditate. It's a basic skill that anyone can use.

MEDITATION FAQs

Q. How often should you meditate?

A. A goal of every day, for 15–20 minutes, is a good baseline to work from. Don't overdo it, as longer periods of meditation can begin to reverse its beneficial effects or produce unwanted emotional experiences. It is best to stick to one, or at most two, 15–20 minute sessions a day.

Q. How do you get ready to meditate?

A. Before starting, choose relaxing music or sounds to establish a thoughtful and tranquil mood. If you prefer, you can continue your preferred music or sounds during meditation to enhance the experience.

Q. What do you do now?

A. In order to meditate successfully, you sit quietly, somewhere quiet and peaceful if you can, and concentrate entirely on a word, sound, image or other point of focus.

Q. What can I focus on?

A. You can meditate by focusing on a word, phrase, short poem or sound; this is known as a *mantra*. Alternatively, you can focus on a picture or image; this is known as a *mandala*, and is often circular or has circles within it, as mandala means 'circle' in Sanskrit. Before you start to learn to meditate, it is important to decide whether to use a mantra or mandala.

Q. Can I pray when I meditate?

A. If you have a faith or belief system that involves praying, you can pray while meditating as an alternative to using a mantra or mandala.

Point to remember

Your attention is likely to wander at first when you meditate, but don't give up if it does. Just notice quietly what has happened and then return your thoughts, without forcing them, to your point of focus. Practice is needed for a new skill like this, and you'll gradually be able to meditate for longer without being distracted. Give it time. It's worth persevering.

USING A MANTRA

Choose one of these mantras or affirmations:

▶ Calm

▶ Shee-reem

▶ One

▶ Om.

Make yourself comfortable, in a sitting position. You're aiming to relax deeply but not to fall asleep. If you like, play some relaxing music or sounds. Before meditating, allow time to begin to unwind slowly. Let it happen in its own time.

When you're ready, start saying your mantra quietly and effortlessly. Stretch its sound out gently and rhythmically, and repeat several times. When you feel ready, whisper the mantra. Then when it feels right, just think it silently to yourself, and eventually think it silently with eyes closed. If you prefer, you can repeat the mantra out loud (chant).

Don't be distracted or annoyed if your attention wanders; simply return your thoughts quietly to your mantra.

Slowly build up your meditation session from a few seconds to a maximum of 15–20 minutes, once or twice daily.

USING A MANDALA

Choose one of these mandalas:

▶ a picture, tapestry or drawing of a very patterned and brightly coloured circle

▶ a loved one's face

▶ an open water lily on a pond.

You can meditate by focusing on the actual object, a picture of the object or by imagining the mandala in your mind's eye.

Make yourself comfortable, in a sitting position. You're aiming to relax deeply but not to fall asleep. If you like, play some relaxing music or sounds. Before meditating, allow time to begin to unwind slowly. Let it happen in its own time.

When you're ready, bring your thoughts to your mandala, whether real or imagined. In your own time and without forcing it, allow your attention to slowly leave behind everything else, as you focus completely on every detail of the mandala: texture, shape, colour, light and shade, movement.

Don't be distracted or annoyed if your attention wanders; simply return your thoughts quietly to the mandala.

Slowly build up your meditation session from a few seconds to a maximum of 15–20 minutes, once or twice daily.

MINI-MEDITATIONS

According to Prof Carrington, 'mini-meditations' can make meditation work for you even if you don't have much time. Several shorter sessions of meditation every day, each lasting two to three minutes, can also bring great benefits. This approach can be very helpful for people who are on the go all the time and find their tension level rising as the day goes on. By regularly meditating, their mind and body relaxes every few hours, meaning that tension no longer builds throughout each day. Most people have several two to three-minute opportunities in their day: break times at work, waiting for your lunch order to be prepared, in a queue, on a bus or train, before the others arrive for a meeting, standing at the photocopier, waiting for an appointment etc. Quick relaxation techniques like mini-meditations fit into these moments neatly provided you chose a method that suits where you find yourself.

Next steps

The key points covered in Chapter 11 are:

✵ **finding out what stress is**
✵ **ways to listen to and understand your body**
✵ **ways you can tackle stress**
✵ **what to do if you have panic attacks**
✵ **how music, sounds and images can ease stress.**

Part 3:

Helping yourself

11

Coping with stress, anxiety and panic

Some people struggle to accept they are depressed. Depression doesn't always feel the way we expect it should. This is especially the case for the many who experience anxiety or panic attacks along with the depression, because it feels as if anxiety is the main problem. As mentioned earlier, the combination affects around seven out of ten depressed people. Since many medications help both depression and anxiety, there is clearly a relationship between anxiety and depression. It is also extremely common for stress to cause both anxiety and depression. So there is a kind of roundabout of symptoms, and it's often not clear where you actually stepped on to it. This chapter will consider how stress, anxiety, panic and depression can often occur together, and how to tackle the stress that often triggers the other three.

How do you feel?

1 In the past week, how stressed did you feel on a scale of 0 (not at all) to 100 (maximum possible)?

2 In the past month, what situations, if any, have caused you (or a loved one) stress?

3 In the past week, how anxious did you feel on a scale of 0 (not at all) to 100 (maximum possible)?

4 What do you think being assertive means? (Choose any that apply.)

a Not sure
b Standing up for yourself
c Getting what you want, no matter what
d Being aggressive
e Respecting yourself as well as other people

5 How many people do you feel you can talk to about feeling stressed or down?

a None
b Not sure
c One
d Two
e More than two.

What is stress?

Stress can make people anxious or panicky, or both, especially if it goes on for a long time rather than being a short-term experience, such as for exams or a problem that resolves itself within a few days or weeks. If stress goes on for a month, and then another and another, longer-term effects such as depression can arise. This is understandable; coping every day with a stressful situation that doesn't get any better is discouraging, distressing and lowers self-esteem. It also drains the body, making you vulnerable to viruses and infections, as the immune system loses its strength. And feeling fed-up and down now and then can easily drift into feeling down all the time, until you can become medically depressed.

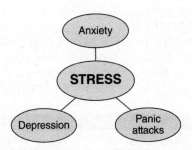

Mythbuster

Myth: A little stress is good for you.

Truth: It's not. That's like saying a little bit of toothache is good for you and only the full-blown thing is bad. All stress is bad for you. It's being motivated, energized and interested that is good for you, and we all need some of that, not stress.

People can become tense or stressed if they feel a lack of control and too much pressure. This can be brought on by relationship or family problems, money worries or being bullied at work or school. Sometimes it can just be that there's a lot of changes occurring in your life, or endless annoying everyday hassles. Generally, people can become stressed if they feel:

▶ threatened or trapped

▶ that they might make a fool of themselves

▶ overwhelmed

▶ unable to cope as well as they want to

▶ dissatisfied or unhappy

▶ unsure or unfamiliar with a situation.

Symptoms of stress

Stress upsets your normal, finely balanced body 'chemistry', and brings about changes in your usual behaviour and thinking processes. This produces a range of noticeable and unpleasant symptoms.

Body	Emotions	Behaviour
Sweating	Panicky	Restlessness
Headaches	Fearfulness	Can't sleep/very sleepy
Churning stomach	A sense of unreality	Eating too much/too little
Palpitations	Irritability	Forgetfulness
Tiredness	Mood swings	Making mistakes
Dry mouth	Anxiety	Poor concentration
Muscle tension	Depression	Nail-biting
Weight gain/loss	Negative thinking	Change in usual behaviour
Trembling	Feel worthless	Indecision
Frequent minor illnesses	Feel out of control	Anger

Stress shows in your breathing. It speeds up your breathing rate, sometimes just by few extra breaths a minute. Breathing using your upper chest increases too, replacing more relaxed abdominal breathing. Changes in your breathing cause changes to how you feel, and this happens very quickly. You can feel faint and tense, tingling in your fingers, poor concentration and your mind can go blank, making you forget what you were about to say.

Point to remember

You might find it difficult to cope if you try to make too many changes at once. So don't try everything suggested in this chapter at the same time. Choose one thing, and when you've got that sorted, move on to something else.

Dealing with stress

First, decide whether you can do something about the reason for the stress.

If you think you can do something about the reason for the stress, then give it a go. You could also find someone with the expertise to advise you about it if that would help. Do all you can to cushion yourself from the effects of tackling the cause, and build your resilience too.

If you're not sure whether you can do something, seek expert advice and support to help clarify the situation. A chat with an objective and supportive third party could help you see what the main issues really are and what, if anything, you can do to improve the situation.

If you are unsure why you feel stressed, the cause may be your lifestyle or general approach to life or business. If so, this chapter should help you to explore this.

MAKE TIME FOR RELAXATION

How you choose to relax will depend on your preferences, but allowing your body to chill out completely at least once every day soothes your nervous system and encourages recovery. A quiet walk, relaxing music, a lazy bath are just a few everyday ways you can do this. Special relaxation techniques are also useful because they are quicker to do, and they can usually be fitted into your day anywhere and in any situation.

Try these techniques and see which works for you.

- ▶ Complete body scan – breathe in gently while silently scanning your body to find where the tension is. Then, as you breathe out, release any tension you've found. Repeat once.

- ▶ Puppet power – take in a really deep breath, hold it for a second or two, then let it go in a huge sigh, dropping your shoulders and slumping your whole body like a puppet whose strings have suddenly been cut. Repeat once.

Tension, anxiety and stress all make you breathe faster because your body think's there's a problem and is preparing itself for rapid action. You might only be taking a few extra breaths a minute but that's enough to alter how you feel and how you think about life. Breathing normally again can help to relieve many of the symptoms of stress, to reduce tension and anxiety and to make you feel more content.

Try the following technique to slow and regulate your breathing, yet still remain alert. Focus your thoughts on your breathing, then begin to count slowly backwards from 10 to 0, saying the next number silently each time you breathe out.

Mythbuster

Myth: Deep breathing is good for you.

Truth: No, it is natural, normal breathing which is good for you. Breathing that is concentrated in the upper chest and/or is too fast, even by a few breaths a second, is bad for you as it upsets the body chemistry's delicate balance. Taking lots of deep breaths can cause panic attacks, angina pain, back pain and other problems.

TAKE BREAKS

When people are stressed, a common, often unconscious, reaction is to miss out breaks: having coffee from a machine while you work; eating at your desk or while shopping or walking to your next appointment or meeting. This makes a kind of sense – you can get more done and meet the deadline or get to an appointment on time – provided it's only a short-term measure. If you then resume your usual routine, there's no harm done. But if non-stop working slips into becoming the norm, i.e. happening most days or, worse, every day, then your system can't take it, and your body and mind will begin to suffer.

Mythbuster

Myth: If I skip lunch, I'll get more done.

Truth: Skipping breaks is a counter-intuitive choice. You don't actually get more done if you skip lunch and your tea or coffee breaks, even if you drink lots of coffee or high energy drinks to keep you going or grab a sandwich on the go. Apart from the health problems related to irregular eating and too much caffeine, your body will be working well below par for most of the day owing to tiredness. If you haven't eaten, your blood sugar levels will be well below the optimum for any kind of task, and your concentration, memory and problem-solving abilities will decline with each hour that passes. If you take regular breaks and eat properly, over the average day you'll get more done, and it will be done better. Even a five-minute complete break in a stressful morning can work wonders.

MANAGING YOUR TIME

Skipping breaks is usually accompanied by poor time management. Often this is unthinking, because our body is already stressed and is pushing us in the wrong direction. Low levels of the 'fight or flight' response makes us rush into everything, talking quickly, eating little and working for too long, instead of forward planning or thinking things out properly. To counteract this tendency:

▶ don't set unreasonably tough targets for yourself – you can often be the one who does this to yourself, so cut yourself some slack

▶ keep lists of jobs to be done, separating the urgent from the non-urgent

▶ select and prioritize what you do; you can't do it all, so delegate whenever possible

▶ plan your days and weeks in advance and keep a diary

▶ be organized and know where everything is

▶ do one job at a time

▶ say 'No' when you should (more on this in Chapter 13).

Stress is not always caused by being busy and pressed for time. Many people feel stressed because they have too much time to fill, perhaps through loneliness, poor health, disability or unemployment. Or they used to be busy but are not any longer, perhaps following retirement or redundancy. You can do something about the problem in situations like this. Ways to take control and make things come to you, or go out to find them, are covered in Chapter 13.

LIFE IS FOR LIVING

There are many easily made adjustments to the way we live our lives that make stress easier to cope with. This is called building resilience, or cushioning. Here are some general tips; note in your journal any you think might work for you, and try the changes one at a time when you feel ready.

▶ Eat a healthy and well-balanced diet.

▶ Don't skip meals, especially breakfast and lunch.

- Avoid too much food or drink containing caffeine, e.g. cola, coffee, chocolate.

- Don't use alcohol or other substances to help you sleep or relax.

- Get plenty of restful sleep. Use relaxation techniques if you have difficulty getting off to sleep or you wake during the night (see Chapter 6). If you have a late night, allow time to catch up on missed sleep.

- Regular physical activity or exercise that you enjoy and which fits in with your lifestyle releases tensions and promotes calmness and feeling good.

- Make time for hobbies, interests and leisure pursuits.

- Do regularly the things you enjoy. 'Me-time' is a must, not selfish; everyone around you will benefit from a happier, more relaxed you.

Quick fix: Relaxing by numbers

Slowly and silently count down from 10 to 0. With each number, imagine yourself unwinding, releasing tension, letting go and relaxing your entire body a little bit more. Repeat if necessary.

COPING WITH PANIC ATTACKS

If you have panic attacks brought on by stress, look out for the first signs of an attack. For many people, this is a lurch in the stomach, an anxious thought or the heart rate rising. Whenever you notice the sign or signs, pause briefly and use any relaxation technique that you can do easily and without being noticed. When you feel calmer again, continue with what you were doing.

THINKING YOURSELF CALM

Your thoughts, attitudes and basic beliefs can contribute greatly to how stressed you feel. In Chapter 5 we explored examples of this, such as using words like 'should' or 'must', tending to blame yourself when things go wrong or taking a negative view of life. Once you're aware of this process, it becomes possible to change it. We all know people who seem able to cope with anything, and others who crack at the slightest problem.

Knowing why this is, and learning how to adapt our thinking and language for the better, is part of cognitive therapy.

Point to remember

Stress is not always connected with bad things. Even happy events – a forthcoming wedding, the birth of a baby, buying a new house – can be stressful. This is because even good things involve change, and even welcome change is stressful.

ASSERTIVENESS

Assertiveness is often wrongly confused with aggressiveness and self-centredness. But assertiveness is about quiet confidence, respecting yourself and others, knowing and being able to express your needs, and being able to compromise with others. Everyone's behaviour varies from situation to situation, but if a lot of what you do is not assertive, this can cause stress. If you are not assertive, you are likely to be manipulative, aggressive or inclined to passively give in to others. Chapter 13 covers how to be more assertive.

A PROBLEM SHARED...

'No man is an island', as John Donne said. It's human nature to need someone who cares about us and who is interested in what we do. When we're stressed, this support helps us through it. Having the caring support of others can even prevent us from feeling stressed in the first place, and contributes much to our resilience to stress. A problem shared really is a problem halved, provided you share it with someone you can trust.

These are the main sources of support for most people:

▶ your partner, if you have one

▶ family

▶ friends

▶ colleagues at work, or the confidential counselling service provided by some employers

▶ support groups or others in your community.

Information about support groups in your local area can be found in local directories, libraries, advice centres and on the internet (see also Appendix 4).

Your thinking space

Make a plan of action for yourself to improve your support network – you could include this in your journal.

✳ How much social support do you feel you can rely on? Score this on a scale of 0 to 100, where 0 is none and 100 is the maximum.

✳ Where is the support coming from? Which individuals? Which organizations? Where else?

✳ Would you like to have more social support? Where would you prefer that to come from? How could you put that in place?

Stress caused by work

If your work or work situation is the cause of your stress, think very carefully before tackling the source of the stress head-on. There could be repercussions for your job or future career, unfair though those might be.

A common way to deal with workplace stress is to build up your resilience, i.e. to cushion yourself from the stress using the methods covered so far, especially relaxation, breaks, social support, a healthy lifestyle and leisure activities.

Stress caused by work is increasingly common nowadays, and comes from a variety of sources. Look at the list below and see if there are any that affected you:

▶ long hours

▶ tight deadlines

▶ difficult people

▶ job insecurity

▶ juggling family and job

▶ incompetence in others

▶ working conditions

▶ isolation

▶ conflict with others

▶ role uncertainty

- being a workaholic
- business problems
- cramped conditions
- bullying
- being overloaded with work
- noise
- heat/cold
- constant change
- low pay
- shift work
- travel to work
- expected to arrive early
- expected to stay late
- demands on home life
- always on duty
- the responsibility
- moving home a lot
- poor communication
- being away from home a lot
- lack of confidence
- lack of control
- no job satisfaction
- unlikely promotion
- personality clash.

There can be other, less direct causes.

- Sometimes a job isn't right for you because it doesn't suit your personality. If this is the case, the solution might be to change your job. If you can't do this, building up your resilience to stress is the best answer.

- Perhaps you have a low tolerance for stress; many people do. If this is the case, can you find a less stressful job? If you can't, building up your resilience is again the best solution.

Consider also whether learning new skills might make a difference. Would a course in assertiveness, confidence-building, mindfulness, NLP skills, time management, team-working, delegation or IT be helpful? Are courses like this available to you either at work or from adult or higher education?

Another possibility might be confidential counselling or coaching, if this is available through your employer. Many employers now provide this entirely independent of the workplace.

Quick fix

In your own time, take a gentle breath in for a slow silent count of 1...2...3. Then, in your own time, breathe out to a slow and silent count of 1...2...3. Continue gently breathing in and out to this rhythm for two to three minutes.

Resilience

When stress first became a major issue some decades ago, the approach to managing it was to deal with the problems immediately before us. The advice was to slow down, learn to relax and breathe properly, look for and deal with stressors etc. Now, we've moved on to place the emphasis instead on stress prevention, stress awareness and building resilience to stress.

Chapter 3 looked at how to be more resilient to depression. Those strategies can be added to strategies for fighting stress to create the 20 key strategies below for building up your emotional resilience to stress and depression.

1 Relax your mind and body sometime every day.

2 Aim for a lifestyle that includes regular exercise, leisure time, and 'me-time'.

3 Eat healthily, avoid too much caffeine, and don't skip meals.

4 Scan your body for stress and tension regularly each day.

5 Share your troubles with a good support network.

6 Know that you are not a victim, and that you can take control and make changes to improve things.

7 Avoid hurry and rushing.

8 Don't use alcohol or non-prescription drugs to combat stress or depression.

9 Don't give up easily. Know that sometimes all that's needed is a little more effort.

10 Adopt a positive attitude to life.

11 Have inner strength, self-esteem and self-respect.

12 Be able to think about and solve problems.

13 Respect your own needs and those of others, know how to compromise, and be able to say no when you want to.

14 Recognize that everyone can make mistakes, and know how to learn from them.

15 Have friends who are positive, up-beat and supportive.

16 Have a sense of humour, and be able to laugh at yourself sometimes.

17 Take regular breaks, and get a good night's sleep.

18 Accept offers of help, or ask for help when it's needed.

19 Work out your priorities, and be organized; know where you are, where you want to go and how you plan to get there.

20 Have a sense of purpose.

Next steps

The key points covered in Chapter 12 are:
* understanding mood swings
* reasons for mood variations
* why moods can vary during each day
* how what you eat can affect your mood
* how to help yourself to have fewer mood swings.

12

Coping with mood variations

This chapter focuses on mood, a central feature of depression, and what a depressed person can do to lessen the impact or the extent of mood variations. Medication or talking treatment can take several weeks to achieve its maximum effect, and self-help can be particularly useful in the period before the benefit starts to be felt.

How do you feel?

1 Over the course of an average day, which of these describes your mood? (Choose all that apply.)

   a Same all day
   b Starts low and gradually gets better as the day goes on
   c Starts quite well, but gradually gets worse
   d Can change very suddenly maybe once a day
   e Changes more than once a day

2 Have you tried anything to cope better with your moods, apart from medication?

   a Yes
   b All the time
   c Sometimes
   d No

3 If you answered a, b or c to question 2, has anything you've tried been effective and if so, what?

4 If you answered d to question 2, why was this? (Choose any that apply.)

   a Didn't know I could do anything for myself
   b No energy to try anything
   c Hadn't realized I had mood swings
   d Not sure

5 Have any of these affected you in the past month? (Choose any that apply.)

   a Very low mood
   b Feeling it's all my fault
   c Mood swings
   d I never know where I am
   e Sudden tearfulness
   f Moods affecting my relationships
   g Feeling I should be more in control.

Mood swings

Having a 'low mood' is typical of depression, but there can also be mood swings, where you have a sudden change of mood;

these swings are not as great as in bipolar disorder, but they are definite swings. The swing can be from feeling down and depressed to suddenly feeling cheerful and enthusiastic; likewise, the mood can suddenly go in the opposite direction, from feeling up to feeling down.

I'm OK one minute

I feel down the next

If something disappointing or disagreeable happens, even if it's something relatively trivial – a sad ending to the film you're watching, a sad news story – you can suddenly feel sad and tearful. Things that others might not even notice can be upsetting and leave you worried, angry or in tears; or can make you feel delighted and wanting to laugh. Or your mood can change for no reason at all.

This unpredictability is the confusing aspect of mood swings. Depression can make you touchy and oversensitive, and neither you nor those around you are sure of how you might react to everyday events. This can mean that your life may be spoiled by moods, arguments and upsets.

Quick fix

When you're feeling down, try to do something active – housework, gardening, washing your hair, aerobics, dancing, walking, whatever. Being active helps to lift your mood.

Mood variations throughout the day

Many people with depression find that their mood varies throughout the day, but tends to be at its worst at the same time each day. It is common to feel worse in the morning and to improve as the day progresses, so that by late afternoon you can wonder whether you'd imagined how depressed you felt earlier in the day. You can even talk yourself into believing that you are 'just not a morning person'.

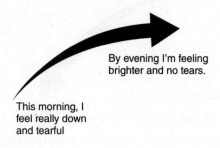

By evening I'm feeling brighter and no tears.

This morning, I feel really down and tearful

Case studies

Lorna

Lorna is a teacher in her mid thirties, who lives with her husband, also a teacher. She wakes quite early most mornings and can't get back to sleep, as she finds herself going over and over the day ahead in her mind, but in a negative fearful way. She wants to pull the covers over her head and stay in bed where it's safe. She forces herself out of bed and then the day just clicks gradually into place and moves on, taking her with it. By lunchtime, she's usually feeling much brighter, and by home time she's looking forward to the evening ahead.

Lee

Lee has just had his 27th birthday and is celebrating two years with his girlfriend, Su-lin. Though he wakes every morning feeling a bit down and anxious, he feels he can cope with the day, and gets up without too much of an effort to start his day. But as the day goes on, he finds anxiety and low mood getting worse until after he has his evening meal, when things improve again.

Try some of the following suggestions to help disperse early morning heaviness, lack of energy and negative feelings.

▶ Try relaxing your mind and body before you get into bed and when you lie down to sleep (see Chapter 6 for ideas).

▶ Think about or write down three good things that happened to you during the day.

▶ Get a natural daylight bedside lamp to put on when you wake up, or the sort of alarm that raises the light level to mimic sunrise before waking you with a bell, buzzer or more natural sound of your choice. Once awake, open your curtains and soak up the natural daylight; even on a cloudy or rainy day there is enough light to make a difference. This prompts your brain to release the chemicals that can lift your spirits.

▶ If getting out of bed is difficult, make just the first movement towards this without worrying about the rest – sit up and push back the covers, have a stretch and yawn etc. This will make the next step much easier, and then the next, and so on. Then get into a warm shower, with some scented shower gel or soap. This will wake you up and wake your senses for the day ahead.

▶ Don't skip breakfast. Try to eat something, preferably something healthy but nice. Indulge yourself by buying the fruit, bread etc that tickles your tastebuds rather than that week's special offer at the supermarket.

▶ Keep your mind active over breakfast. Talk to whoever shares breakfast with you, even if it's only a short conversation – the weather's always a good topic with adults, while you can ask children about the day ahead, or their friends. If you live alone, read a magazine you really like or a gripping book. Listening to a breakfast news or chat show works well too. Let your thoughts be drawn outwards to the world around you and away from too much introspection.

Point to remember

Everything in this book should help you to become more at ease with yourself and make mood swings less of a problem. You can try to lessen their impact yourself even if you're taking medication – self-help shouldn't conflict with the effects of your medication.

Other mood problems

Moods and mood variations can cause problems. These are often related to those around us, especially those closest to us. Do any of the following apply to you?

▶ guilt

▶ feeling nobody understands

▶ regret

▶ cutting yourself off from people

▶ hurting those you love

▶ hating yourself

▶ aggression

▶ sudden outbursts

▶ violence

▶ damage to property

▶ broken relationships

▶ ups and downs

▶ rows all the time

▶ anger

▶ unpredictability.

What causes people to have these moods and the problems that come with them? Is there more to it than being depressed? Let's look at reasons, other than depression itself, for extremes of mood and mood swings. Some of these reasons are relevant only to women, but most can apply to men too.

Understanding your moods

Somehow a better understanding of why you feel the way you do can have a calming effect on your mood. It can give you a kind of release and let you off the hook of your own self-imposed guilt. It can also help your relationships if your partner, family, friends and colleagues have a better understanding too. Explain matters to them when you are having a good day, or lend them this book.

Point to remember

Factors other than depression can cause moodiness, so it's worth trying to do something about these too.

STRESS AND MOODS

Chapter 11 explained the importance of relaxation and managing stress and anxiety, and how this can have a great impact on depression. Relaxation and stress management can also ease moods and mood swings, and make panic attacks less frequent and less severe. It's important for those who are working to make sure that there is an overall balance between work and a home life and leisure interests.

DIET AND MOODS

One of the main reasons for people being moody or getting angry seemingly out of the blue is because their blood sugar level is low. Low blood sugar makes you more likely to feel irritable, bad-tempered or angry, especially if the drop is sudden. To avoid highs and lows in your blood sugar level, eat small regular meals and avoid food and drinks that are high in sugar; these give a quick energy boost followed by an equally quick drop in blood sugar levels. It's OK to have a healthy snack between meals too.

Research findings by the mental health charity MIND support the following 'Food for Mood' tips for lowering anxiety and keeping your mood up-beat.

▶ Eat a healthy, well-balanced diet.

▶ Don't skip meals.

▶ Avoid eating on the run or 'grazing' throughout the day. Taking time to eat regular meals calms your digestive process.

▶ Avoid sugary snacks as they cause peaks and troughs in your blood sugar levels, which affect your mood, and produce cravings for more sugar. Read food labels, as many seemingly healthy snacks have a high sugar content. Snack instead on nuts, raisins, sultanas, dried apricots, a banana, an orange, grapes or other fruit, oatcakes or a pure fruit smoothie.

▶ Avoid long gaps (two to three hours at most) without eating. Eating little and often maintains a constant blood sugar level, which helps to protect you from tension, anger, frustration and aggression, and gives you energy too.

▶ Don't drink too much coffee or other drinks containing caffeine (e.g. cola, 'power' drinks). Many cold and flu remedies contain caffeine, so a hot lemon for your cold, plus a power drink and some chocolate can give a huge shot of caffeine, making you edgy and nervy.

▶ Choose foods that are digested slowly. These are foods that have a low Glycaemic Index (GI) rating and include wholegrain bread, pasta, nuts, low-fat yoghurt, bananas, apples, apricots, oats, fruit juices, porridge and basmati rice.

Eating a healthy, well-balanced diet with regular meals can help to even out your moods. 'Well-balanced' means low in sugar and fat and high in fibre. But be careful to keep the balance right – there is evidence to suggest that eating a diet too low in fat can cause low moods, or even depression.

Mythbuster

Myth: What you eat makes no difference to moods or depression.

Truth: There's plenty of evidence that skipping meals and having too much sugar or caffeine will affect your mood, and in the long term this can cause depression. Some studies suggest that foods high in omega-3 fatty acids, such as salmon, walnuts and spinach, can have mood-improving properties, and that if your diet includes a lot of olive oil, you are less likely to be depressed.

RELATIONSHIPS AND MOODS

We all need positive social support, and this is particularly important if you are depressed or prone to moods. Without a supportive partner, family or good friends, moods and depression can be especially difficult to cope with.

Having someone who cares about us and who is interested in what we do can bring great relief in depression. A problem shared with the right person really is a problem halved. If you already have a good support system, make maximum use of it, both as an outlet for feelings and as a source of encouragement. There's no need to feel guilty about doing this; the favour can be repaid some day. If your existing support system needs building up, make a start on that as soon as possible.

Indeed, whatever the state of your support, it's always worth making it stronger. Try this to build up your support network.

▶ At the top of a new page in your personal journal, write 'My support network'.

▶ Fill in down the left-hand side of the page the names of the people you would like to see more of – partner, family, friends, colleagues etc.

▶ What would be your first step for seeing more of each person you've listed? Note your answers down the right-hand side of the page, opposite the person's name.

▶ Are there any organizations or groups you would like to contact? Fill in their names down the left-hand side of the page.

▶ What would be your first step for each of the organizations you've listed? Note your answers opposite the name.

It would appear that even talking to strangers can make us feel better. Recent research at the University of British Columbia found that even a short time spent with strangers tends to improve your mood. The researchers believe this is because we try to impress strangers and so act cheerful even if we don't feel cheerful, but that acting cheerful has the effect of putting us in a better mood.

HORMONES AND MOODS

Pre-menstrual syndrome (PMS) can have a very powerful effect on mood. It can cause low mood, very sudden mood swings, outbursts of anger and irrational thinking. Many an argument happens at this 'time of the month'.

The key self-help strategies are staying fit and eating a healthy, balanced diet, because blood sugar levels and certain key vitamins seem to have a major impact on PMS. Read up on the subject, and speak to your doctor if self-help doesn't seem to be working. Try keeping a diary of your behaviour, moods and other symptoms, such as bloating, breast tenderness and cravings, for a few months before you attend your doctor. There are also helpful medications available if self-help isn't working.

Case study: Katy

Katy was finding her temper and moodiness before her period had become worse since she started a new job in a nearby supermarket. A friend told her that having long gaps without eating had made her PMS worse – something about peaks and troughs of blood sugar levels, she explained. Katy never ate breakfast, so if she went straight to work, she could go for four hours or more on an empty stomach. After she started to have some cereal for breakfast and to eat a few nuts and raisins whenever she could at work, Katy found a distinct improvement in her pre-menstrual symptoms.

The years leading up to the menopause, when periods actually stop, is called the peri-menopause, and during the peri-menopause there can be mood swings. PMS can become more severe during this time, or may be experienced for the first time if someone who has never been troubled by it before. Periods that are heavier than normal or irregular and unpredictable can also leave women feeling on edge, upset and moody. If this becomes too difficult to cope with, your doctor should be able to help. If you find it easier to talk about these things with a woman, make an appointment with a female doctor at your practice.

MID-LIFE CRISES

Many of us, both men and women, find when we reach our late thirties or our forties that we begin to question what life is all about and where we are going. It is a time when we can become acutely aware of ambitions unrealized, or feel that others are doing much better in life. We question what we have achieved so far, whether it is too late to achieve anything else, and wonder what's the point of it all. We may lose our parents or even our partner and suddenly feel there is nothing standing between us and the end of our life. This can leave people feeling scared, vulnerable and lost for a while. Talking things over with a trusted friend or a coach or counsellor can help to deal with these issues.

Improving your moods

The various reasons for mood variations, mood swings and low mood are amenable to self-help. Try some of the strategies below (which include some from earlier chapters); these are particularly good for settling unpredictable moods.

▶ Eat small, healthy, regular meals, avoiding sugar and caffeine.

▶ Don't blame yourself for your moods – it's mainly your body causing these.

▶ Be nice to yourself. You are a good human being.

▶ Be active for at least half an hour every day. Walk, run, go to the gym, dance, play with the kids, whatever you enjoy.

▶ Keep busy. But pace yourself and have breaks and rests too. Breaks should be a priority, not at the bottom of the list. After all, how often do we reach the bottom of the list?

▶ Laughing and feeling cheerful lift your spirits. So keep to hand your favourite comedy film, compilation or stand-up, or a book of amusing anecdotes or family pictures that always make you laugh. YouTube has a constantly updated supply of funny video clips.

▶ Keep handy by your usual seat the activities that occupy your mind when you need distraction – a magazine to read, Sudoku or crossword puzzles, jigsaws, craftwork, the phone numbers of friends etc.

▶ Even if you're not a dedicated gardener, plant something and watch it grow. It can be anything – seeds, herbs or bulbs – in the garden or greenhouse if you have one, or in pots in the house, conservatory or window box.

▶ Relax every day for a minimum of five minutes, and preferably for 30 minutes to an hour. Use a CD or DVD to help, or try some of the techniques in Chapter 6. A quick relaxation technique, one which only takes seconds or a couple of minutes to do, if used regularly throughout the day, can have an amazing effect.

Next steps

The key points covered in Chapter 13 are:
✳ **ways to cope if you feel lonely**
✳ **how to rebuild confidence and self-esteem**
✳ **how to be assertive**
✳ **what to do if you get angry**
✳ **how the internet can help.**

13

Other self-help techniques

Issues that come up again and again when I talk to people who are depressed are lack of confidence, loneliness, feeling angry with yourself or other people, and not being able to speak up for yourself when you need to. This chapter looks at how to deal with these issues, as well as telling you about the help and information that can be accessed using modern technology such as the internet.

How do you feel?

1 How assertive are you? Rate yourself to be on a scale of 1 to 10.

2 Do you sometimes or often feel angry, even though you may not show it?

3 Do you ever feel lonely? If so, what brings on this feeling?

4 How easy do you find it to say 'no' to people? Rate yourself on a scale of 1 to 10.

5 Thinking about your confidence and self-esteem, do you feel:

   a Over-confident
   b That it's not a problem
   c Not confident enough
   d I have no confidence at all
   e Don't like myself much
   f Can be arrogant sometimes.

Dealing with loneliness

Being depressed can be a vicious circle. It is not only an unpleasant way to feel, but it also has the effect of shrinking your comfort zone, as you begin to feel less confident about going out or socializing. Lack of energy and feeling down make it harder still. It's easy in this situation to lose touch with friends and have less and less going on in your life, which then makes you feel even more down.

The support of friends and family can help when you're depressed. Yet even if friends visit, you have little to say when you see them, and they don't know what to say to you; people can find it difficult to know what to say to someone who is depressed, which may stop them visiting or make them avoid you in the street or the shops. This vicious circle can go on for weeks or months, and when you begin to feel better, you can find that you have to rebuild your social life again.

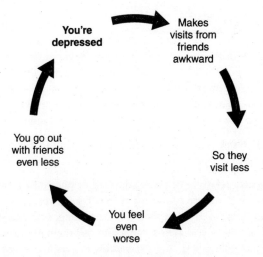

You're depressed → Makes visits from friends awkward → So they visit less → You feel even worse → You go out with friends even less → You're depressed

Some suggestions follow about how to keep in touch with the outside world when you're depressed and how to kick-start your social life if you need to, so that you can join in again with old friends and make new ones. When you feel you are part of the world again, your mind will have something to focus on other than negative thoughts and worries.

You can do most of these things alone, as many people do, or you can recruit a supportive friend to join you. Start small with something you feel ready for, then move on a step when you feel it's time. Note the ideas you like in your personal journal, deciding whether to try them 'now', 'soon' or 'later'.

► Put yourself in situations where you can easily become involved in conversations and activities. Go for a short walk, go shopping, catch a bus or train, visit a museum or exhibition, take a course, watch street theatre or other street activities.

► Take the initiative and talk to other people, rather than waiting for them to talk to you. Have an opening few words ready, perhaps about the weather or how busy/quiet things are, as these are usually good ways to start a conversation. Talk to the shop assistant, the postman, the delivery man.

- Check your email or surf the internet in a local internet café instead of at home.

- Go to a local shop every day for a newspaper or some shopping. You'll be amazed at how you get to know the people you meet regularly on the way, if you go at the same time every day. That's how my brother met his wife, and they've just celebrated their silver wedding anniversary!

- Read your book or magazine in the park among other people instead of at home.

- Go to see relatives or friends instead of phoning or emailing them, or ask them round for coffee. Don't worry too much about what to say. Let them do the talking, nod every so often to show you are listening and ask them about what they are telling you. Suggest making it a regular event, say every fortnight, so that you don't have to make arrangements from scratch every time.

- Look in your local paper for events you can attend. Although I live in a rural area, according my local paper today there is a guided woodland walk, a fireworks display, a farmers' market, a stand-up performer at a comedy club, a music society production of *West Side Story* and a football match within easy reach. All of these will be attended by many people, some of whom will also be on their own.

 Quick fix

When you're out, relax your shoulders, hold your head high, put on a smile or say 'hello' even if you don't feel like it, and see how others react. I guarantee you'll get smiles and greetings back. And you have the bonus of increased serotonin from the smiling, the daylight and the walk.

Building confidence and self-esteem

When you're depressed, your confidence and your self-esteem can hit rock-bottom, which makes everything harder: going out, staying in, gathering the energy to make a phone call or send a text. Here are ten suggestions that might help; as ever, take one careful step at a time.

Don't be so hard on yourself. None of us is perfect: we all have weaknesses; we all make mistakes. It's not always *your* fault either – often someone else is to blame, or it's just bad luck or a situation you can't do anything about.

Remember you are a human being and you have rights. Here are just a few of them:

▶ you have the right to your own opinion

▶ you have the right to be treated with respect and as an equal

▶ you have the right not to be bullied or put down

▶ you have the right to be listened to

▶ you have the right to fail or make mistakes

▶ you have to feel angry sometimes

▶ you have the right to try again.

People in authority are just people. If you get nervous around authority figures like doctors, managers, council officials or teachers, remember that they are just people, with homes, families and friends. It can also help if you picture them in their underwear or in silly clothes!

Be a good listener. You don't have to come up with clever things to say – just be a good listener! Listen to other people, show an interest or ask them about themselves. People love that, and will like you for it.

Walk and talk confidently, and you'll feel confident. Before you go into a room, pause for a second to take a deep breath, then with your head up and your shoulders and body relaxed, open the door confidently. Use a warm, calm and low-pitched voice, speak at a medium pace, and smile. Make regular eye contact. It doesn't matter if it's an act; if you appear confident, people will treat you as if you are confident, and then you'll feel more confident. And gradually the act will become reality.

Learn to relax. If you're stressed, angry or upset, relaxing your body will calm the situation and your thinking, and will help you to cope better. Try taking a deep breath and then let all the tension go from your body as you breathe out. Repeat if necessary.

Remember 'I'm OK, you're OK'. Keep in mind that you're an OK person, and most other people are OK people too. Mutual respect, in other words.

Don't forget you have lots of strengths. Life experiences can point up our shortcomings and weaknesses very effectively. We're only too aware of these and can feel very guilty about them. But we all have strengths too – that includes you!

Look around you! Turn your thinking outwards and look around you at where you are, at other people and what's going on with them. This helps you to look both interested and interesting. When you're anxious or down, it's easy to retreat into your head but this makes everything more difficult. So turn your eyes and thinking outwards and take in the view.

Remember that most people are not as confident as they look. Many people, despite their confident appearance, are quite shy inside; there are lots of people out there who are faking it! So don't feel intimidated by someone who acts as if they own the place.

 Quick fix

At the head of a new page in your personal journal, write 'Strengths'. Being honest but *not* modest, write down your strengths. Ask a relative or friend for help – their view of your strengths might surprise you.

Assertiveness

Difficult situations often arise from people not being able to communicate their needs and wishes to others, either in relationships or at work, or both. Assertiveness is about being able to express what you feel or what you want in a calm and confident but unthreatening way.

But assertiveness is also a widely misunderstood concept, so here is an exercise to clarify what assertiveness is. Read the descriptions below and decide which people you think are being assertive.

▶ People who make sure they get what they want no matter what

▶ People who are aggressive to others

▶ People who dominate or control other people

▶ People who find they can never say 'no'

▶ People who cannot speak to others about their own needs

▶ People who use put-downs or sarcasm

▶ People who can't compromise

▶ People who don't listen to other people's point of view

▶ People who get their own way by making others feel guilty

▶ People who cannot give criticism without devaluing the other person.

As you may have realized, *none* of these people are displaying assertive behaviour. Assertiveness is often confused with aggression. You sometimes hear people being told that they 'need to be more assertive!' by people who really want them to be more self-centred, pushy or aggressive. But being assertive doesn't mean being aggressive, selfish and overbearing. Quite the opposite; assertiveness is about treating yourself and others with respect.

A low level of assertiveness usually indicates that someone behaves passively for much of the time; they are not able to say 'no' to people and are generally a bit of a dogsbody. This pattern of behaviour is usually linked to a lack of confidence and low self-esteem, often arising from childhood or previous life experiences. Low levels of assertiveness can, however, also result in a tendency to dominate others or to sometimes be aggressive, sulky or manipulative.

If you're not being assertive, you may be behaving in one or more of the following ways.

Passive	Apologizing all the time
	Putting everyone else first all the time
	No confidence
	Unable to say 'no'
Passive-aggressive	Behaving passively most of the time but flipping occasionally into aggression as frustration builds up – the 'worm turning'
Over-confident/Arrogant	Know-all
	Nothing's a problem
	Loud
	Full of ideas
	One-upmanship
Manipulative (also called 'indirect aggression')	Manipulating others to get your own way, by making them feel guilty or by sulking, sarcasm or put-downs
Aggressive	Threatening
	Overly competitive
	Angry
	Intimidating
	Domineering
	Abusive
	Must have own way
	Must win
	Must be right

However, if you behave assertively, you:

► know your own needs

► are aware of your own strengths and weaknesses

► have genuine respect for yourself

► have genuine respect for others

► are open, direct and honest whenever appropriate

► know how to compromise.

Assertiveness is based on the idea that everyone is equal, that everyone has the same rights and that we should all have respect for ourselves and other people. We should all be able to communicate as equals.

These behaviours are not entirely distinct from one another, but should be seen as part of a continuum; aggressive behaviour and passive behaviour are the extremes, with assertiveness in the centre.

| Passive | Assertive | Aggressive |

Quick fix

Be nice to yourself. Depression can make you care less about your appearance and taking a shower or bath can seem an effort. Women, if you can afford it, how about having your hair washed and blown dry at the hairdresser's every few weeks instead of doing it yourself at home? Men, how going for a wet shave, or a regular swim and maybe a sauna?

BECOMING MORE ASSERTIVE

Improving your assertiveness skills may help you to cope better at work and in dealing with loved ones, friends and neighbours. If you want to pursue this, there are many books on the subject, and many workplaces and local colleges provide courses.

Here are some suggestions for helping yourself to increase your assertiveness; as ever, take one careful step at a time.

▶ Keep to any point you're making – don't let others distract you from it.

▶ Keep your head up, maintain frequent eye contact and a confident posture.

▶ Aim to come over as warm and friendly.

▶ Speak slowly in a warm and calm voice.

▶ Never act aggressively, or shout or threaten people.

▶ Have confidence in yourself, and don't be timid.

▶ Remember your rights as a human being. You have the same rights as everybody else.

▶ Value and respect yourself, and value and respect other people.

▶ Be ready to say 'no'. Don't give reasons or 'excuses' unless you really have to – you don't have to explain to everyone.

▶ Adopt an assertive posture – shoulders relaxed, walk and sit tall.

▶ Don't over-apologize.

▶ Think before you speak.

- Ask for time to make a decision if you feel you need it.

- Don't sulk or make people feel guilty.

- Be open to negotiation and compromise.

Mythbuster

Myth: Confronting an angry person is the best way to calm things down. You can't allow such behavior.

Truth: How would you respond if you were angry and someone confronts you about it? Imagine it. Would you become calmer, or would you feel attacked? Would your anger disappear or would it escalate? Most of us become angrier, not calmer, if we're confronted about being angry.

Dealing with anger

What about when it all gets too much, and anger wells up inside you? Here are some tips for coping with your anger.

- If you're getting angry, don't let your anger build; this isn't good for you and never makes anything better.

- If you're getting angry, try to keep your voice relaxed, low-key and soft. It's hard to get angry with a soft, warm voice.

- Eating small, frequent, healthy meals helps prevent highs and lows in your blood sugar level, which will help to reduce mood swings and relieve the tension and frustration that can make anger likely.

- Being active and exercising regularly makes you more relaxed and less likely to react to situations with anger.

- Remember that it's not people or events that make you angry, it is your *reaction* to the people or events that makes you angry.

- Get to know what triggers your anger. As soon as you are aware of getting angry, use relaxation or calming techniques to counteract the feeling, calm your breathing and relax tense muscles.

- Listen and communicate actively with others. Be interested in what they are saying. Allow your body to be relaxed and at ease. Practise accepting valid criticism or saying 'no' in a calm and even-handed way.

▶ Try replacing angry thoughts with a calming image, such as lapping waves, and imagine your anger as a candle that can gently be blown out.

▶ Take time to think before you respond to people – don't leap straight in. Don't jump to conclusions, and don't 'mind-read' other people's thoughts and intentions – you're usually wrong. Give people a chance to explain.

▶ If your anger is getting the better of you, make an excuse and leave the situation for a few minutes, allow yourself to calm down by using a breathing exercise or relaxation technique, and return when you feel calm.

Mythbuster

Myth: It's better to express your anger than hold it in.

Truth: Most people think that you should let out your anger so that it doesn't build up inside. Wrong. Even though films such as *Anger Management* and many self-help authors suggest punching pillows, tearing up old newspapers or using shouting to release anger, all the research shows that expressing your anger makes it bigger and more aggressive. That's why if you let go and throw one ornament, you're likely to continue until you clear the shelf, and then move on to whatever else comes to hand. It's also why you should leave a room if you feel you're going to lose it and lash out at a loved one. Many assaults are made much worse by this effect, which can take even the perpetrator by surprise. One reason this myth arose is that people usually feel better after they have expressed their anger (unless someone or something has been damaged), but anger subsides on its own anyway after a while.

Finding help

The NHS and its regional offshoots have comprehensive and easy-to-use websites which provide extensive specialist information, including diagnosis opportunities and the option of speaking to someone for advice. The starting point for accessing these is the UK-wide website at www.nhsdirect.nhs.uk

Depending on where you live and the interests and specialisms of nearby doctors and other health professionals, one or more of the following may also be available.

► Special software programs preloaded onto terminals that you can use at a local surgery. These are computerized treatment programmes which you use over a number of sessions, along with written information to take home with you.

► A terminal in a health or community centre, or other public place, with access to online NHS information and support.

► Other special websites and downloadable apps (see Appendix 4). Some of these are available on prescription in some parts of the UK. Bear in mind that these change all the time, with new ones constantly becoming available. Choose carefully – make sure you're using a reputable source.

Mythbuster

Myth: The older you get, the more irritable you will become.

Truth: It's the other way around – as people age, they report fewer negative emotions and greater emotional control.

Next steps

The key points covered in Chapter 14 are:
* **how becoming more positive can help**
* **what happiness is, and how to be happier**
* **the importance of self-respect and how to build it**
* **ways you can laugh again**
* **working out what's important in your life.**

Part 4:

Moving forward

14

How to be happier

We probably all remember stories from our childhood which ended with 'and they all lived happily ever after'. For many people, that is their main aim in life – to be happy, and to stay that way. When you are depressed, happiness is an emotion that seems so out of reach. Seeing people smiling and laughing around us can be really hard to take. It's especially difficult if you have a job which requires you to appear cheerful, such as a tour guide, beautician or receptionist. If you're depressed, you can become very good at pretending to be happy, hiding your real feelings behind a happy face. So what is happiness? And what do you have to do to be happy?

How do you feel?

1 Think of a time you felt happy as an adult. What words would you use to describe that feeling?

2 Can you recall any times when you felt happy as a child?

   a Yes
   b No
   c If yes, when and why?
   d If no, what stopped you feeling happy?

3 On a scale of 0 to 100, how happy you have been in the past month?

4 If you could make three wishes for things that would make you happy, what would they be?

5 When was the last time that you:

   a Smiled
   b Laughed inside
   c Giggled
   d Laughed out loud
   e Felt happy.

Why seek happiness?

Since the 1970s, there has been an increase in depression in every wealthy country in the world. Currently, there's considerable interest worldwide in assessing how happy we all are, and how we can become happier. In 2012 the first-ever UN Conference on Happiness was held in New York, attended by 600 delegates.

The reason for this interest is that research has shown that 'happy' children have more friends, are better problem-solvers and are more independent and enthusiastic. Research also shows that being happy has many benefits for adults too, because 'happy' people:

▶ are healthier

▶ cope better with illness

▶ live longer

▶ donate more to charity, both in money and time

- have more empathy with people in need
- are more productive at work
- persevere with things more
- are more positive.

What is happiness?

This is a simple question, but one that it's really difficult to answer, as happiness is a highly individual experience. How happy you feel tends to depend on your age, general health, quality of life and current circumstances; it would seem irrelevant to ask someone living in a refugee camp, or in the midst of armed conflict if they are happy. Even in a peaceful and prosperous country such as ours, how you experience happiness will be different from how I do. Happiness is difficult to describe and even harder to measure. To make it easier to assess and research formally, happiness is now often defined as being part of 'mental well-being', something a questionnaire can measure fairly accurately. 'Mental well-being' is defined as 'feeling good, and functioning well', a description that most of us can relate to.

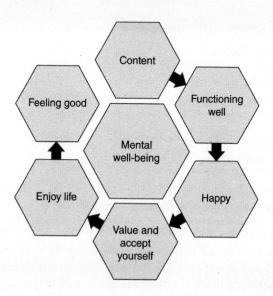

Mythbuster

Myth: It's better not to talk about being depressed. It just makes it worse.

Truth: Many depressed people, as well as some of their friends, do avoid talking about it. It's 'the elephant in the room'. Some depressed people behave this way because they believe this myth and hope their problem will go away if they ignore it. Unfortunately, this can also stop them seeking help from their doctor. Some friends and family also believe this myth and discourage the depressed person from talking about it. Repeated negative ruminations about your depression may not be a good idea, but constructive discussion with friends and family and, certainly, working with a therapist to learn new skills can do nothing but good.

Your happiness quotient

Chapter 8 described how to carry out a life audit covering different aspects of your life. Your life audit scores give an overview of your life, showing which parts of it you are most and least happy with; you could call it your happiness profile (HP). If you add up your life audit scores, this gives your happiness quotient (HQ), scored out of 100. Here is an example.

Name: Parminder, mother of two, aged 29	
Area of life	Happiness profile (score from 0 to 10)
Your family	8
Personal relationships	9
Where you live	5
Friends and social life	2
Work or career	4
Money	5
Your health	8
Fun and recreation	5
Personal growth and learning	5
Inner soul and spirit.	7
Your happiness quotient	58
Which aspect would you like to improve first?	Friends and social life
How will you start to do this?	Go to local parent and toddler group.

Try this for yourself in your personal journal. You can also identify one area of your life you would like to improve, and how you could make a start to this. Look back at this on a regular basis, say once every few months, to check on your progress; you can gradually improve those areas of your life that you feel would most improve your general sense of happiness and well-being.

Quick fix

Think of something small you can easily do to help a friend, and do it. It makes you feel good too.

HOW HAPPY IS BRITAIN?

An opinion poll in 2005 showed that Britain's happiness levels are declining. The poll found that the proportion of people saying they are 'very happy' had fallen from 52 per cent in 1957 to 36 per cent in 2005. Polling data throughout the 1950s showed happiness levels higher than they are today, so Britain is less happy than in the 1950s despite being three times better off; increased prosperity does not seem to have brought increased well-being.

Here are some other poll findings.

▶ 43 per cent said their neighbourhood was less friendly than 10 years ago.

▶ 48 per cent said that relationships were the biggest factor in making them happy, with health coming second at 24 per cent. Fewer than 8 per cent said work fulfilment was an important source of happiness.

▶ two out of 10 people spoke to only one or two friends each week, and one person in 25 talked to no friends at all.

▶ nearly 50 per cent of married people said they were 'very happy', but only 25 per cent of single people said the same.

Quick fix

If you feel the beginnings of a smile, do all you can to encourage it. A smile makes you feel better, and everyone around you too.

'DESERVING' HAPPINESS

You may feel you don't deserve happiness, anyway. It's common to feel that way if you're depressed – it's often part of the condition – but sometimes the belief has become a part of you. Sometimes you have been told this often enough to believe it, or it arises from something that's happened in the past. If this applies to you, much of what you've read so far should be helpful, especially chapters 2, 3, 5 and 8. Because everyone deserves happiness. None of us is perfect, and we only have one life. Being happy ourselves makes everyone around us feel better too. If you're still not sold on doing it for yourself, do it for them.

Quick fix: Happy moments album

Collect photographs of loved ones, of happy events, of 'you've been framed' type moments, or photos that just make you smile. Either put these in an album or on the computer, perhaps as a screensaver, so that you can look at them any time you need cheering up.

What makes us happy?

This question is easier to answer if we think about 'mental well-being' rather than 'happiness'. The NHS Choices website suggests that there are five steps to mental well-being, and with this will come happiness. The effectiveness of each of these steps is supported by research evidence.

Step	How to achieve this
1 Connect	Keep your close relationships strong.
	Reach out further to your community and the world (see Chapter 15).
2 Be active	Find activities you enjoy, and build them into your life (see Chapter 6).
3 Keep learning	This doesn't have to involve study or qualifications; it can be as informal as you like.
	Boosts self-esteem and gives a sense of purpose. Makes us more optimistic, and gives satisfaction.
	Helps us connect with others.
4 Give to others	This has been shown to help create positive feelings.
	Acts of kindness, large or small.
	Helping and supporting other people.
	Working together with others to achieve something.
5 Take notice	This is also known as mindfulness (see Chapter 7).
	Pay more attention to the present moment.
	Notice your own thoughts, feelings and sensations from moment to moment.
	Notice details of the world around you.

All the research suggests that what we do and think has more impact on our happiness and well-being than what we possess. My mother used to say that life could be good even without much money 'just as long as you have enough to oil the wheels'. In other words, as long as you can pay for the basics of life, how much money you have has little bearing on how happy you are; who you are and how you live your life is more important.

Mythbuster

Myth: Depression is just feeling fed-up or blue – it's a normal part of life.

Truth: Saying depression is like feeling fed-up or blue is like saying that a stubbed toe is the same as a broken leg. We can all be fed-up now and then, but the feeling only lasts an hour or two, or a few days at most. And being fed-up doesn't makes us cry, feel anxious or be unable to eat or sleep properly. Depression, on the other hand, can cause all of these things, and go on for weeks.

How to be happier

A constant theme in discussions of happiness is the human need for meaning and purpose, and how important this is to mental well-being. Chapter 15 looks at this in more detail.

Quick fix

Think of a place you are always happy... then close your eyes and take yourself there in your imagination.

Laughter is also a good 'medicine'. Humour helps people feel more relaxed and boosts their resilience to stress, which also enhances their resilience to depression. Laughter gives a physical and emotional release, relieves tension and promotes relaxation.

Even a smile will cause the brain to release endorphins, the feel-good neurotransmitters, so it pays to bring as much smiling and laughter into our lives as we can manage. Here are some suggestions on how to do this.

- Choose funny or light-hearted television programmes and DVDs.

- Cheer someone else up. The American writer Mark Twain said that this is the best way to cheer yourself up.

- Read amusing books, rather than thrillers or horror.

- Loosen up and let your hair down – splash about in the pool or bake something messy with the children.

- Have a party for your birthday, for a special holiday or just for fun. All of these create a positive and cheerful atmosphere.

- Make friends with positive, happy people, and spend time with them.

Quick fix

According to the Scottish Association for Mental Health, research has shown that doing an act of kindness once a week over a six-week period can increase your well-being. So why not:

✳ smile at the next person you see

✳ volunteer to work for a charity

✳ check on a neighbour who might need help.

Next steps

The key points covered in Chapter 15 are:

✳ **how to stay motivated**

✳ **understanding setbacks**

✳ **breaking the cycle – knowing what keeps depression going**

✳ **thinking about the way ahead – making short-term and long-term plans**

✳ **your 'best bits' from this book.**

15

The way ahead

Writing this book has been an important journey for me, and I hope I've made it easy to follow and useful for you. I've covered everything that I thought might help someone who has a mild depression, is in a moderate or deeper depression or is witnessing this difficult illness in a partner, relative or friend.

To end our journey, I'm going to reiterate here some of the key points from the book, look at how your personal journal can help you in future and suggest ways to motivate yourself on those days when life seems to be an uphill struggle. Finally, we'll look at how to make a recurrence of your depression less likely.

How do you feel?

1 You're now at the last chapter in the book. Did you:

   a Read the whole book straight through to here
   b Skim the book to here
   c Look at this chapter first
   d Dip in to the chapters which interested you

2 What do you want from this chapter?

   a More answers or information
   b Encouragement
   c Enthusiasm
   d More understanding about depression
   e Closure
   f Something else

3 Are you feeling any of these right now? (Choose any that apply.)

   a Fed-up
   b In low spirits
   c Down
   d Depressed
   e None of these

4 Have you felt any of these in the past few weeks? (Choose any that apply.)

   a Tearful
   b No energy
   c Over-reacting to everything
   d That no one understands
   e None of these

5 How clear do you feel today about the way ahead?

   a Have a rough idea of where I'm heading
   b Not very clear at all
   c Yes, I feel I know what's ahead for me
   d Not sure yet.

You were asked questions 3 and 4 before, in Chapter 1. What were your answers to these questions then? I hope this chapter provides everything that you've said you're looking for in question 2. And the intention of this last chapter is to help you with question 5, to help you to look forward, and think about what you want to be ahead for you and how you can make that happen.

Purpose and meaning in life

Purpose and meaning are themes that come up again and again in research into happiness. When you're depressed, you find yourself asking, 'What's the point?', and 'What does anything matter anyway?', and that's what makes purpose and meaning important.

Good mental well-being largely comes from feeling that you know what you're doing, where you're going, and why, i.e. having a purpose and a meaning to your life. Or to be more precise, recognizing what that purpose is and being able to see it clearly. Depression can make us 'partially sighted', or even completely 'blind' when it comes to our strengths and the purpose and meaning of our lives, even though it's obvious to everyone around us. Recovering from depression, however you achieve this, is to a large extent about taking off your blindfold and seeing your life for what it really is; there's so much more going for you than you thought!

Reading this book shows that you already have a purpose in life, which is to overcome your depression. This is a good starting-point from which to accomplish what you want to achieve. Sometimes it seems too great an effort, but on the days when you feel up to it, it is an effort worth making. You may have ups and downs along the way, but the main thing is to keep going, keep improving your overall health and well-being and working towards overcoming your depression.

Quick fix
Cherish your courage, and keep it close by for when you need it. Reading this book is a sign of your courage – carry on using it to help you get better. Keep a tight hold of it, and don't let it go.

WHAT IS IMPORTANT TO YOU?

As part of establishing what gives purpose and meaning to your life, it is useful to reflect on some of the bigger issues in life and how important these are to you.

Work through the following list and rate each according to how important that item is to you, in general, most of the time. Note in your personal journal a score between 0 and 4 for each item using the scale below. Don't spend time on soul-searching about the answers – your first thought is probably the most accurate.

0 Doesn't matter at all to me

1 Not very important to me

2 Quite important to me

3 Very important to me

4 Extremely important to me

Subject area	Rating	Subject area	Rating
Independence		Friends	
Learning		Adventure	
Variety		Love	
Having children		Your family	
Helping others		Having a partner	
Novelty		Marriage	
Work		Power	
Approval		Integrity	
Leadership		Success	
Happiness		Freedom	
Intimacy		Respect	
Your home		Achievement	
Security		Excitement	
Challenge		Passion	
Affection		Money	
Status		Travel	

Now, have a look at your scores. Are there any surprises?

▶ Which score 0 and 1, the least important to you? Are they similar?

- What about the highest scores? How many score 4? What are your highest scoring items? Are they similar?

- Do your highest scoring items have enough priority in your life right now?

What people really need

The psychologist Abraham Maslow designed a hierarchy of human needs, with the basic bodily needs (such as food and drink) at the bottom, physical safety needs next, and our higher order needs (such as our need for love, self-esteem and a sense of belonging) above that.

If we don't have food, drink and shelter, we soon die, so in those circumstances we are not concerned about higher order needs, only about our safety and our children's. But if we have food, drink, safety and shelter, we can begin to care about being loved and valued and having a sense of belonging.

The diagram of Maslow's hierarchy of needs below shows how satisfying the needs that are most urgent, or low order, moves our needs up a level.

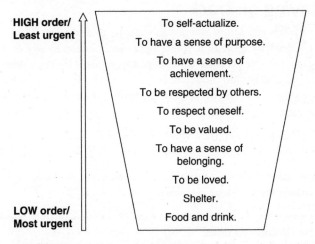

HIGH order/ Least urgent

To self-actualize.

To have a sense of purpose.

To have a sense of achievement.

To be respected by others.

To respect oneself.

To be valued.

To have a sense of belonging.

To be loved.

Shelter.

Food and drink.

LOW order/ Most urgent

The highest order of need, to self-actualize, means to realize oneself to the fullest, to make real or 'actual' all of your potential and be all you can be. This may take a lifetime for some to achieve, and many of us will never meet this need; we may never even have the chance to think about it because throughout our lives we are entirely taken up with meeting lower order needs.

This table describes these needs in more detail.

Self-actualization	Fulfilment, realizing your full potential; following your own passions and interests; being able to express yourself; having a sense of who you are; being all you can be.
Artistic needs	Beauty, order, creativity
Thinking needs	Knowledge, understanding, novelty, intellectual stimulation
Purpose needs	Long- and short-term goals and direction
Esteem and respect needs	Competence, confidence, approval, recognition, prestige, self-respect, respect from others, status, being valued, achievement
Belongingness and love needs	Giving and receiving love and affection; belonging; having roots; affiliation
Safety needs	Security, comfort, freedom from fear
Bodily needs	Food, water, air, sex

Staying on track

Even when you know where you want to go and why, it can be particularly difficult if you're depressed to keep to any sort of plan. In your personal journal you have three lists of things that you want to do 'now', 'soon' and 'later'. Here are some suggestions to keep you persevering with these and to help you get where you want to be.

▶ Tell someone you trust about the plans you have – then they'll ask you about them, making you more likely to act on them.

▶ Use your personal journal as a reminder and as a kind of route map to where you want to be.

▶ Don't take on more than you can cope with. Try only one or two things at a time.

▶ Find a positive and encouraging friend who has time to be a mentor. Ask them for support and encouragement, and to be a friendly voice at the other end of the phone.

- Set up reminders on your mobile phone, tablet or iPad to encourage you.

- Make what you want to do realistic and achievable.

- Note down all the benefits you (or others) will gain from your plans and all the negatives that will disappear. Read these often, and especially any time that you're tempted to give up.

- Set specific targets; you can't act on vague general ideas.

- Check your progress at the same time every week.

- Give yourself small rewards when you have worked hard or made a difference.

Quick fix

Be aware of your inner strength. It's there, no matter how weary you feel right now. Close your eyes for a few moments and connect your thoughts with the strength that's deep inside you.

Key strategies for overcoming depression

This book has covered a lot of ground. Although it's good to have an abundance of information, ideas and approaches to overcoming depression, it can create another problem for you – deciding where to start! It may help to know my six key strategies for overcoming depression; chapter references are also given so you can refresh your memory on particular topics.

Strategy 1: Thinking (see also chapters 5, 7, 8, 14)

- Think positively and challenge any negative thoughts.

- Live in the here and now, and be 'mindful' whenever you can.

- Avoid dwelling on negative thoughts – turn your mind to something else.

- Find ways to encourage happiness and mental well-being.

Strategy 2: Mood (see also chapters 8, 12, 14)

▶ Watch out for thinking that pulls down your mood.

▶ Take action if you notice signs that your mood is getting low.

▶ Build mood-lifting activities into each week.

▶ Use 'anchoring' to improve mood.

▶ Work on being happier.

Strategy 3: Lifestyle (see also chapters 3, 5, 6, 11)

▶ Be active every day.

▶ Relax your mind and body deeply and often in a way that suits you.

▶ Eat regularly and healthily.

▶ Get some daylight every day – or even better, some sunshine.

▶ Find new things to do that you enjoy.

▶ Build your resilience to stress and depression, but keep stress to a minimum when you have a choice.

▶ Keep a good work–life balance.

Strategy 4: Socialize (see also chapters 6, 11, 13, 14)

▶ Spend time with positive, cheerful people.

▶ Build up supportive relationships with trusted friends or family, a counsellor, a church leader or a good self-help group.

▶ Consider getting a pet. A dog, cat or similar pet gives companionship and unconditional love.

Strategy 5: Choose your life map (see also chapters 5, 7, 8, 13, 14, 15)

▶ Work out where you want your life to go, and how to make that happen.

▶ Be realistic about life and love (e.g a violent or cheating partner, nasty neighbours etc)

▶ Sort out any problems that are getting you down.

- Be ready to make changes when you need to.

- Don't forget you can learn new skills if you want or need them.

Strategy 6: Seek medical help when you need to (see also chapters 4, 5, 6, 9)

- Know when you've reached the point when you need help.

- Don't feel guilty about seeking help – depression is an illness like any other.

- Use medication and talking therapy if you need to.

- Talk to others with depression if that helps.

Staying well

This aspect of dealing with depression doesn't appear in many books on the subject. Yet depression can and does recur for many people, so it's just as important to prevent its return as it is to overcome it in the first place.

Don't drift along – always be aware of the bigger picture and what's going on in your life. When making a life choice, think about whether it will create too much stress or increase your risk of failure or loss. Plan ahead to spread any extra work or ask for some help.

Take notice if one of your triggers has occurred (there is a list of possible triggers in Chapter 1), and take preventative action – don't just keep your fingers crossed that you'll be OK. For instance, don't take on too much at work, avoid sad films, take exercise, relax your mind and body, get plenty of rest, be mindful, practise positive thinking, mix with cheerful people, join a support group, talk to your doctor or therapist. Building up your resilience like this will make you better at coping with stress as well as helping avoid depression.

Be alert to the subtle changes in your thinking or behaviour that indicate that you may be going into a depressive episode. I have noticed that if I am laughing a little too much at jokes, picking fights with my husband or sitting on the sofa daydreaming, then my mood is on its way down. Everyone has their own signs, and if you notice any of yours, take action straight away to reduce the potential for stress or for feeling overwhelmed. These are the harbingers of depression, not the full-blown illness, so there is probably still time to nip things in the bud.

Point to remember

If you've taken on too much, let some of it go again. Be kind to yourself and make life a little easier. Put off making big decisions for a while. This isn't being selfish – keeping yourself well will benefit not only you but everyone around you. Depression is an illness, and you need to keep your serotonin level right in just the same way that a diabetic needs to keep their insulin level right.

Here's a summary of the key aspects of avoiding a relapse, bringing together points covered in this and earlier chapters.

▶ The best way to avoid a relapse is to make sure you recover from depression fully. No matter how you're treating it, keep going until you're completely well.

▶ Watch for your triggers (see Chapter 1), and early signs, so that you can catch a reoccurrence early, before you have actually become depressed.

▶ NICE currently recommends that you continue on medication for a minimum of six months after symptoms have gone, and then cut down the medication gradually, with a doctor's guidance, over a period of at least a month. Some drugs, such as Paroxetene, leave the body faster than others, so they should be reduced more gradually than, say, Fluoxetine, which is lost much more slowly.

▶ Don't be in denial about your depression and negative feelings, or the chance of relapse. Keep your wits about you.

▶ Learning to handle stress better and building up your resilience (see Chapters 3 and 11) will help prevent a relapse.

▶ Cognitive behaviour therapy (see Chapters 5 and 6) will give you new tools to help overcome and avoid depression.

- If you've had two or more moderate or severe episodes of depression in the past, NICE recommends that you stay on medication for at least two years after you feel well again. Your doctor may also offer other, more long-term support, so keep in touch with them.

- If you've had three or more severe episodes of depression, using mindfulness (see Chapter 7) or following a course in mindfulness-based cognitive therapy can reduce the possibility of another episode.

- Once recovered, look after yourself. Eat well, sleep well, live well, love well. Make this your new life, as much a part of your everyday routine as brushing your teeth.

- Keep using your personal journal.

Your personal journal

Research shows that a personal journal can be very helpful in overcoming depression. You may have been making use of your personal journal since Chapter 1. If you haven't, then you can start at any time, but it's entirely up to you whether you use a journal or not – and it's OK to miss a few days occasionally.

Here's a summary of the key aspects of using a journal, bringing together points covered earlier in the book.

- Each day, make a note of how you feel (this can be as short or as long as you like). You can use a word or phrase, such as 'sad', 'down', 'more positive today', 'good', 'fair', or an appropriate 'smiley' (or emoticon). Or if numbers appeal more, score your day on a scale of 1 to 10, or 1 to 100. When you look back, it helps you to see where the good days and bad days were, and you may be able to see reasons for these. Sometimes it can show you that you've had more good days than you thought; it's easy when you're depressed to remember only the tough days.

- Every evening, take a few moments to think back over your day and write down three good or positive things that happened. These need not be anything big or special:

a text from a friend, something interesting in a magazine, something delicious to eat, a glimmer of sunshine after the rain, your dog running to meet you when you came home. Start by doing this every day, then just three or four times a week. At the end of the week, read over all the positive things you've written. Studies have shown that doing this regularly can lift your mood significantly.

▶ I suggested that you make lists under three headings. You can continue with this for as long as you want, or even make a fresh start. The three headings are:

▷ Changes and techniques you're starting *now*

▷ Changes and techniques you want to start *soon*

▷ Changes and techniques which you'll get to *later*.

▶ It helps to include a page reference with each item, to make these easier to find later on. As you progress through the lists, you can move items from 'soon' to 'now', or from 'later' to 'soon'.

▶ Look at your life audit (Chapter 8) and your happiness audit (Chapter 14). Identify one area of your life that you would like to improve, and decide how you could make a start to this. Check your progress on a regular basis, say once every few months, so that you gradually improve those areas of your life that you feel would most improve your general sense of happiness and well-being.

And finally

Our journey together through this book is coming to a close but I hope that you will continue to be aware of a 'virtual me' still beside you, supporting and encouraging you. You now have the equipment you need for the road ahead: a greater understanding of depression and its causes, and a range of strategies for finding your way over the bumpy stretches of the road. This book will always be there too, to refer to if the going gets rough and you need to remind yourself of what to do.

As you know from reading about my experiences, I am living proof that there is life and happiness after depression and that you can begin to cope again, even with the toughest of circumstances. I know many, many others who have lived through and moved beyond the grip of depression. Go on, it's your turn to join us.

Appendix 1:
Helping someone
with depression

(For contact details, see Appendix 4)

Throughout this appendix, 'friend' means the depressed person, although they might be a partner, family member, friend, colleague etc.

Recognizing when someone is depressed

As well as experiencing depression myself, I've also looked on as depression took hold of someone I loved; I'm not sure which is worse. Watching a loved one with depression is a challenging experience, evoking a mixture of anger about their suffering and frustration and powerlessness in the face of the illness.

Chapter 1 outlines the general signs that someone is depressed. If for the past month your friend or loved one has experienced three or four of those symptoms on more days than not, they may be depressed and should see a doctor.

If you're not sure whether or not they are depressed, they should see their doctor anyway for a check-up. Depression doesn't always express itself in easily identifiable ways, especially if it's mild. But mild depression is still depression and needs to be dealt with.

What to do if someone is depressed

Being depressed saps your energy, and it can make you withdraw into yourself and push others away, especially those you care about the most. Your friend may be bad-tempered and sullen, have quick-fire mood changes or other symptoms of depression you'll find described in Chapter 1. Bear in mind that these behaviours are not deliberate but part of the illness, and that your friend can't stop themselves from behaving in ways that afterwards they will probably regret bitterly.

Probably the most valuable thing that you can do is encourage your friend to see the doctor if they haven't done so already. Try to be positive and reassuring rather than pushy, and explain gently and sympathetically that something can be done to make them feel better.

If your friend has already been diagnosed, don't feel you have to cope with the situation on your own. You can suggest your friend sees the doctor again if you feel it's needed. Don't agonize over whether this is really necessary; it's best to err on the side of caution – a doctor will not complain if a consultation wasn't really essential.

Spend time with your friend, talking, walking and doing things they enjoy.

Listen when your friend wants to talk. Even if they go over the same stuff, and you've heard it all before, listen with interest. Resist the temptation to judge. What they are saying really matters to them, and showing you care enough to listen supportively is hugely therapeutic. Allow them to get the negative stuff out, as that makes it easier for them to leave it behind and talk about everyday matters.

Don't give advice unless asked for it, and don't feel you have to offer solutions to their problems and worries. Most depressed people just want a friendly, non-judgemental ear. If you can see something obvious that might help but that your friend is missing, suggest it carefully and diplomatically at the right moment.

Encourage your friend to be reasonably active rather than spending most of the day 'having a rest'. Physical activity shouldn't be excessive, though, as the tiredness that depression causes is very real. But a good balance of rest and activity, combined with keeping busy and contact with friends, family and the world around them, is the best help for someone who is depressed.

Don't be scared to ask how they are feeling.

Find out all you can about depression and how it is treated so that you can understand what's happening to your friend, and explain things to them when the time is right. You can also remind them of new techniques they have learned in therapy and encourage them to make use of these.

Get to know the health professionals and others who are concerned with your friend's care or treatment.

Carers can provide understanding and acceptance that it may be difficult for individuals to find elsewhere.

Stay open and honest with your friend.

Lend a hand with the chores and shopping if needed, but only when your friend is clearly not up to it. The tiredness is real and everything can seem too much of an effort some days. But if they are able, get them involved so that they are contributing something, no matter how small, to whatever you're doing.

Provide emotional support and encouragement.

Look out for signs of setbacks, encourage them to take their medication and perhaps go with them if they have an appointment with their doctor or to attend medical or therapy appointments.

Having a friend who is depressed can be difficult for you to cope with, so look after yourself too. Be careful not to take everything on yourself; find ways to share the load with as many other people as you can. Ensure that you have support yourself and people who can listen to your frustrations and anxieties, perhaps a good friend or a local support group.

Care for the carers

If you find yourself the main carer for someone with depression, coping with the kind of symptoms described above can be distressing and even shocking, leaving you feeling helpless and frustrated. You might even feel angry and resentful, and experience a sense of loss for the friend you used to have, now changed almost beyond recognition. You can also feel the loss of the relationship you had before, with all that had meant to you. The person affected can even push you away – when we're depressed, we often hurt those we love the most. Sufferers are drowning in a sea of misery and want to hit back at someone; those you love are the safest people to hit out at because they are least likely to retaliate, and they often provide unconditional love.

Carers sometimes feel their needs have become invisible and that their world revolves around the depressed person. It's not selfish for a carer to want their needs to be met or to turn their attention elsewhere occasionally. Keeping yourself fit and well is of crucial importance; not only because you have the right to make the most of your own life, but also because if you become ill or exhausted, you won't be able to help anyone else. You'll feel you've let your friend down, and they'll feel even more guilty because of how their depression is affecting you.

So don't feel bad about taking time off to rest and have your own life. Try to maintain a balance, and make sure you do all the things that are needed for your well-being, such as having breaks, taking whatever help or respite is available, going out and doing enjoyable things, and having a laugh sometimes. You will feel better if you are able to rest, socialize and eat properly, and you'll be a better carer, with more energy and enthusiasm to offer.

Some areas have befriending services for people with depression. These can give carers a respite, as well as giving your friend a regular visit from a different face with fresh conversation and opportunities to get out and about when they feel up to it.

There may also be formally organized respite services in your area which will provide you with regular short breaks, and even a longer break for a holiday. Many areas also have a carers' support group which can provide services and resources ranging from emotional support to information, advice and leisure facilities. You should be able to find out about these services through your local authority or doctor (see also Appendix 4).

You may qualify for a state carer's allowance. Your local carers' group, social services department or Citizen's Advice Bureau should be able to advise about this.

Appendix 2: Self-harm and suicidal thoughts or behaviour

(For contact details, see Appendix 4)

Self-harm

People who harm themselves are not always depressed or suffering from a mental illness. Self-harm is thought to be caused by severe emotional distress. This may be brought on by any unbearable situation, and it can start at any age. Everyone's experience of self-harm will be different, as people hurt or harm themselves for a variety of reasons.

▶ It's an outlet for painful and distressing emotions, such as powerlessness or helplessness, lack of control or guilt.

▶ It's an attempt to block out unwanted or painful memories or flashbacks.

▶ It's a way for some people to protect a 'secret self' which is vulnerable and must be kept hidden while their 'social self' faces the world and maintains a charade.

▶ Those who feel guilty or worthless sometimes use it as a way to punish themselves.

▶ Those who feel empty and emotionless use it as a way to 'feel something'.

Examples of self-harm are:

▶ cutting/slashing parts of the body

▶ punching yourself

▶ burning yourself

▶ overdosing on prescribed or over-the-counter medicines

- picking/scratching the skin
- pulling the hair
- banging the head or throwing the body against hard objects.

Sometimes self-harm takes a less direct form, such as:

- binge drinking
- taking drugs
- unsafe sex
- not eating
- driving recklessly.

Although self-harm might occur at any age, in 2012 the Royal College of Psychiatrists estimated that one in ten young people will self-harm at some point. The college also reported that self-harm is most commonly found in:

- people in prison
- young women
- people who were abused as children
- gay, lesbian and bisexual people (probably due to the stress of discrimination)
- armed forces' veterans
- people who feel isolated and alone.

Some circumstances have been identified as possible triggers for self-harming. These are situations that cause intolerable stress, especially if they go on for months or year, with no apparent end in sight:

- relationship problems
- debt
- abuse
- bereavement
- bullying

▶ exams

▶ financial concerns.

There is a common misconception that self-harm is a failed suicide attempt, especially if cutting or overdosing is involved. The mental health charity SANE reports that those who self-harm have more suicidal thoughts and feelings than those who don't, but this doesn't mean that when someone self-harms they intend to die by suicide.

> 'I absolutely don't want to die when I self-harm. I just want the emotional hurt I feel inside to go away…'

According to a study by SANE in 2009, most of the time the majority of self-harmers do not want to die. It would seem that they have persistent thoughts about death or suicide and use self-harm to help manage these thoughts and feelings; self-harm helped them *not* to take their own life.

In a 2009 study by the UK National Self-Harm Network, most of the 758 people surveyed gave self-hatred, anger, frustration and feelings of worthlessness as their main reasons for self-harming; only 4 per cent said self-harming was brought on by suicidal thoughts. Other research puts the percentage of self-harmers with suicidal thoughts higher, at 15 per cent. Regardless of their reasons, those who self-harm are at higher risk of dying from the injuries they inflict on themselves.

There are a number of myths about self-harm.

Myth	Truth
The more serious the injury, the more serious the problem.	There doesn't appear to be any link of this kind. Even the smallest wound or injury may indicate desperate distress.
People who self-harm can easily stop if they want to.	Self-harm is often a way of coping. Without finding a new way to cope, it's going to be hard to stop. Time and support are needed to move away from using self-harm to cope with life.
Harming yourself is attention-seeking.	Self-harm is often seen as a cry for attention, but this is rarely the case. Self-harm is usually a hidden behaviour, with injuries carefully concealed or explained away.

(Continued)

Myth	Truth
Self-harm is the problem; if this stops, the person will be fine.	It's not as simple as that. The reasons for the self-harm need to be resolved to free someone from harming themselves.
Self-harmers must like the pain.	The same argument is sometimes made about victims of domestic violence, and it is just as wrong. Victims of any kind of abuse put up with it for long periods because they are trapped in the situation in some way. Those who self-harm are trapped too, albeit in a different way. Harming themselves is what allows them to cope with their internal distress.

HELPING YOURSELF IF YOU SELF-HARM

There are some excellent organizations that can provide information and support if you self-harm; contact details are given in Appendix 4. They have suggestions for helping yourself on their websites, and there are several helplines too. Here are their key suggestions for helping yourself.

See the bigger picture. Are you harming yourself because you're trying very hard to hold things together and cope with difficult feelings from day to day? Keeping that in mind may help you to be more understanding and accepting of yourself and this behaviour. If you can, allow yourself to begin to think about the feelings and thoughts you have just before you self-harm, it may become possible to think of other ways to deal with these feelings that don't involve hurting yourself.

Distraction. The impulse to self-harm will pass, so when you feel the urge to self-harm, distracting yourself until it has passed is a sound strategy. Here are some of the ways others have found effective and that might work for you too.

▶ Phone a friend, or go round to their place.

▶ Go shopping.

▶ Write or draw something.

▶ Get your nails done or have a massage.

▶ Meditation or relaxation exercises; these can calm the urges and help anxiety.

▶ Bake a cake, muffins etc, or make a meal.

- Watch TV or a DVD or play computer games.

- Take the dog for a walk – borrow a neighbour's if you don't have one.

- Take exercise – whatever you enjoy. This releases endorphins which make you feel better.

Use alternative sensations. If the urge to harm yourself is too strong for a distraction, creating an alternative sensation may prevent more severe harm.

- Have an elastic band round your wrist or ankle that you can snap against your skin.

- Hold ice-cubes in your hand or inside your elbow, which will sting or burn a little.

- Have a cold shower.

- Use a felt-tip pen to make marks or write something on your arm or other part of your body.

Not ready to change? Perhaps you're not ready to take the first step toward recovery yet because you are so drained and exhausted or confused and made anxious by a problem that seems too big to solve. If that's how you feel, here are some ideas.

- To take a step forward, you may need help and support from other people. There are many people out there that you can trust to help you.

- Don't give up if the first person you confide in isn't listening or doesn't help. There are lots of possible reasons for this, none of them to do with you or self-harming; the person you've approached may be too busy or distracted, or not perceptive or informed enough.

- Speak to a family member, your doctor or practice nurse, a teacher, counsellor or friend. Or try a helpline or support group; sometimes the anonymity of an online discussion group makes it an easier place to start.

Getting help. Help and support can come from a wide range of professional people, such as a counsellor, psychologist or therapist. They will understand your difficulties and work with you to find ways to help. If the first person you work with doesn't seem to be right for you, try someone else.

HELPING SOMEONE WHO SELF-HARMS

You may have been shocked or even angry to find someone you care about is self-harming. You may have reacted by hiding the things they've used to harm themselves, confronting them to make them talk about it or insisting they see a doctor. But as harming themselves is what enables them cope with whatever is distressing them, stopping them from self-harming may make matters worse.

Read the earlier sections of this Appendix, as knowledge and understanding will help you to get over the shock and begin to help. The right professional help will eventually be needed in most cases, but for now you can play an important role just by listening and supporting them without blaming or judging them. SANE encourages an approach of 'compassionate acceptance'. Information and support can be found on the internet (see Appendix 4), but here are some key dos and don'ts.

▶ Do make sure the lines of communication are always open.

▶ Do show them you care, and let them know they can talk to you if they want to.

▶ Do let them keep as much control of their lives as possible.

▶ Do find out what they would like you to do to help.

▶ Do read up on the subject and talk to them about the benefits of professional help, coping strategies such as distraction and alternatives to self-harm.

▶ Do let them know you are there to listen any time they want to talk. If the person finds talking to you difficult, give them contact details of support organizations.

▶ Do try to look beyond the cuts and bruises or binge drinking and focus on the person. They are still the same person. If you want to help, be compassionate, non-judgemental and patient with them.

▶ Do try to understand their reasons for self-harming, and that it will be a long and hard journey to recovery.

- ▶ Do be aware that someone will only stop self-harming when they feel ready and able to do so.

- ▶ Do look after yourself too. This whole experience is draining and frustrating. Find support for yourself, and remember you have your own life to lead.

- ▶ Do talk to them when they are feeling they want to harm themselves. Try to understand their feelings, and then move the conversation onto other things – the distractions mentioned above or other topics.

- ▶ Do help them to find out about how to get help – perhaps offer to go with them to see someone, such as their doctor.

- ▶ Do help them to think about their self-harm as a problem to be sorted out like any other problem, rather than as a shameful secret. You can also take some of the mystery out of self-harm by helping them find out more about it.

- ▶ Don't ban any behaviour or express disapproval. It could just force the problem underground and make any further discussion impossible.

- ▶ Don't force them to talk about it. They'll talk when they are ready.

- ▶ Don't watch over them every minute. They need time and space for themselves.

- ▶ Don't pressure them into getting help before they're ready. This takes away their control and will probably backfire.

- ▶ Don't issue ultimatums or make them promise not to do it again – if you do, the pressure to harm themselves will build up all the more.

- ▶ Don't make them feel it's a shameful secret that must be hidden.

- ▶ Don't make assumptions or jump to conclusions. And don't take any action without talking about it with them first.

- ▶ Don't over-react if they tell you they've just self-harmed. Take a breath, hide how you really feel, check if first aid is needed and ask if they want to talk about it.

Suicidal thoughts or behaviour

Talking to someone about suicide *won't* put the idea into their heads or make them more likely to try it. Raising the subject *will* give them the chance to talk about the way they feel, which they've probably been keeping to themselves, and this is more likely to prevent a suicide.

Suicide is rarely a spur-of-the-moment act; there are usually signs in the hours or days before someone take their life. The strongest of these signs is the things they might say, such as that they don't want to live anymore, can't go on, want to finish it etc. Other common warning signs that suggest suicide may be possible are:

▶ previous suicide attempts

▶ being depressed

▶ being withdrawn

▶ getting affairs in order or giving things away

▶ drinking or taking drugs more than usual

▶ agitated, reckless or unusual behaviour

▶ a significant loss or disappointment, or an impending major problem.

People who take their own lives do not always do so because they are depressed.

IF YOU HAVE SUICIDAL THOUGHTS

The Befrienders Worldwide website explains that 'suicide is often a permanent solution to a temporary problem'. The point behind this comment is an important one; being depressed can make things look much bleaker than they are, and problems tend to pass or resolve themselves remarkably quickly. Many people who have had suicidal thoughts are glad they didn't act on them when, a few days or weeks later, everything is looking much better. Many people who kill themselves don't want to die, they just want to stop hurting.

So if you've been thinking about killing yourself, you should **get help straight away** in at least one of these ways.

▶ Talk to a trusted family member or friend.

▶ If it's easier to talk to a stranger, contact a support group or befriending group that can help (see Appendix 4). You can email them if you'd rather not talk or go to see someone.

▶ See your doctor, who will understand and can decide whether you are depressed and provide medication or therapy that will help.

▶ Contact the emergency services.

HELPING SOMEONE WITH SUICIDAL THOUGHTS

If someone you know talks about suicide, you rightly feel you have to do something, but many of us don't know where to start. It is a shock, and both upsetting and confusing to be faced with someone saying they want to kill themselves.

First, collect your thoughts. Then check how serious the risk is and whether an attempt is imminent. Every mention of suicide has to be taken seriously, but whether the risk is high or low at a particular moment determines what you should do.

Severe risk (very high)	Has suicidal thoughts. Has a clear, effective plan. Says they intend to die by suicide.
High risk	Has suicidal thoughts. Has a clear, effective plan. Says they don't intend to die by suicide.
Moderate risk	Has suicidal thoughts. Has a vague, ineffective plan. Says they don't intend to die by suicide.
Low risk	Has some suicidal thoughts. Has no suicide plan. Says they don't intend to die by suicide.

Assess the risk by asking these four questions.

1 Do you have a suicide plan?

2 Do you have what you need to carry out your plan (pills, gun etc)?

3 Do you know when you would do it?

4 Do you intend to die by suicide?

Those at the highest **imminent risk** of suicide will have a specific suicide *plan*, the *means* to carry out the plan, a *time set* for doing it, and an *intention* to do it.

If the risk is severe and imminent, you should:

▶ contact the emergency services

▶ remove any harmful objects

▶ make sure the person is never left alone.

If the risk does not seem serious or imminent, you will want to respond but, unless you're a trained professional, you will probably be unsure what to say. *Doing* the right thing is more important; it's more a question of having the right attitude, and avoiding doing certain things.

▶ Do stay calm, put the person at ease and speak warmly.

▶ Do listen, really listen to their story.

▶ Let them tell you all about how they got to this stage.

▶ They should do most of the talking.

▶ Do be reassuring, and provide a safe and confidential place for them to express their worries.

▶ Do hear the words that the person is using but also look for the feelings that lie behind them.

▶ Do try to understand how they are seeing the world right now.

▶ Do accept and believe what they tell you.

▶ Do let them know you are there for them.

▶ Don't pretend it's not happening and talk about something else.

▶ Don't ask lots of questions, over-analyse their problems or offer platitudes such as 'Cheer up' or 'You'll feel better after a good night's sleep'.

- Don't judge, or give advice or opinions.

- Don't rush them.

- Don't blame or criticize them, or put them on the defensive.

Above all, remember you're not on your own. There is help available locally and also specialist organizations (see Appendix 4) that provide information, advice and support.

Appendix 3: Children and depression

(For contact details, see Appendix 4)

Throughout this appendix, 'child' means anyone under 18.

Signs of depression in children

According to the Mental Health Foundation (2012), around one child in every ten in the UK has a mental health problem, and a 2007 report by the Foundation estimated that anxiety and depression in teenagers had increased by 75 per cent since 1982. The BBC website (2012) reports that about 20 per cent of people aged between 16 and 24 are thought to have a significant mental health problem.

Signs that a child is feeling stressed or depressed are easier to spot if you know the child well, as these will mainly be changes in their usual behaviour, which others wouldn't notice. Even small changes can be significant, so parents and carers should be alert to these. Some children will talk about their concerns and how they are feeling, but others show these through moods and challenging behaviour.

Certain signs are common in children of any age. It's worth seeing the doctor if you notice one or more of the following and the behaviour persists and is unusual for your child:

- appears to be sad
- has become withdrawn
- is less interested in things they normally enjoy
- is unusually worried and anxious
- is critical of themselves and the way they look
- seems frightened
- eats and sleeps much more or much less than usual

- is unusually snappy or angry

- is confused and can't make decisions

- avoids social situations, school, college or work

- behaves in unfamiliar ways

- acts aggressively or in a hostile manner.

The following signs are less usual, and would usually mean that the child should be seen by a doctor immediately:

- seems unable to cope with day-to-day life

- seems so depressed that you are afraid they will harm themselves

- harms themselves.

TODDLERS

Diagnosis by a skilled professional is required. A doctor should be consulted if parents or carers notice subtle changes or more obvious signs indicating that something's not right and there's no improvement after a few days:

- loss of appetite

- tearful and clingy

- has become very demanding

- shows destructive behaviour

- is developing more slowly or taking steps backwards

- wakes up during the night for no clear reason

- has nightmares.

SCHOOL-AGE CHILDREN

See your doctor if you notice one or more of the following signs and they are new for your child but there's no improvement after a few days:

- loss of interest in work and play

- becoming careless and making mistakes

- refusing to go to school

- is irritable and difficult
- lacks confidence
- finds it hard to talk and show their feelings
- stealing
- lying
- missing school.

TEENAGERS

The teenage years are a time of great change anyway, often bringing moods, uncertainty and a lack of communication; these in themselves would not suggest depression. Signs that a teenager may have depression include:

- becoming withdrawn
- not looking after themselves
- losing touch with their friends
- giving up regular hobbies and pastimes
- eating too much or too little
- finding it hard to concentrate
- losing interest in school or work
- low self-esteem
- sleeping badly or sleeping too much.

Causes of depression in children

Just as for adults, life events and loss can bring on depression in children. Sometimes, events that don't seem a problem to an adult can present a major problem for a very young child. Moving to a new home, losing a favourite toy, a new baby in the family or spending long hours with a new childminder can all cause long-term distress. Other circumstances that can underlie depression in children of any age are:

- fear of failing at school
- the death of a much loved pet

- being bullied
- feeling left out
- having a parent who's depressed or anxious
- a serious long-term illness in the family
- feeling lonely
- a new stepfamily
- loss of a parent through family break-up or bereavement
- loss of a loved one or friend
- physical, emotional or sexual abuse
- hearing or seeing frequent arguments
- hearing or seeing domestic abuse.

Helping a depressed child

If you suspect a child is depressed, take them to see their doctor. The doctor won't be annoyed if you're wrong.

Just like adults, children can be prescribed medication and talking treatment. The National Institute for Clinical Excellence (NICE) recommends that antidepressants shouldn't be used for mild depression in children, the same advice it gives for adults. The Royal College of Psychiatrists reports that there is some evidence of increased suicidal thoughts (although not actual suicidal acts) and other side-effects in young people taking SSRI antidepressants. Consequently, most SSRI antidepressants are not licensed for use by anyone under 18, although NICE has said that one, Fluoxetine, can be used in under-18s.

Sometimes family therapy is suggested because it's easier to see the whole picture more easily than by asking the child, who may not be able to put their thoughts or feelings into words or identify the issues and difficulties they are having. Children are very sensitive to what's going on around them, and can detect and become distressed about problems that adults think they don't know about. This kind of therapy also makes it easier for the family to understand how they can best help the child.

Art therapies such as drama, music and dance can be helpful.

If you're worried that a child is self-harming, having thoughts of suicide or making plans to take their own life, talk to the doctor immediately and talk to the child too (see also Appendix 2).

Specialist organizations (see Appendix 4) can provide information, support and advice, including online or by telephone in many cases.

Appendix 4: Useful contacts

An asterisk (*) indicates contacts providing an online self-help programme.

In the UK
GENERAL
Get Self-help
www.getselfhelp.co.uk/links2.htm

An online directory with links to self-help websites and downloadable apps, many of which are free. Some of the paid-for resources are available on prescription in some parts of the UK.

DEPRESSION
Action on Depression
11 Alva Street, Edinburgh EH2 4PH
Information service: 0808 802 2020 (Wed 2–4pm)
E-mail info@actionondepression.org
www.actionondepression.org

Works with and for people affected by depression, providing support and raising awareness of depression and treatment options.

Association for Post-natal Illness
145 Dawes Road, Fulham, London SW6 7EB
http://apni.org

Provides support to mothers suffering from post-natal illness. Increases public awareness of the illness and encourages research into its cause and nature.

Aware
72 Lower Leeson Street, Dublin 2, Ireland
Helpline: 00 353 1890 303 302
www.aware.ie

Provides information and support to people affected by
depression in Northern Ireland and the Republic of Ireland.

Bipolar UK
11 Belgrave Road, London SW1V 1RB
Tel: 020 7931 6480
www.bipolaruk.org.uk

Supports individuals with bipolar disorder, their families
and carers.

Dealing with Depression
www.dealingwithdepression.co.uk/

Online forum (requiring registration) offering help, advice, tips
and links.

Depression Alliance
20 Great Dover Street, London SE1 4LX
Tel: 0845 123 23 20
Email information@depressionalliance.org
www.depressionalliance.org

Provides information, support and self-help groups for people
who suffer with depression, and for relatives who want to help.

Depression UK
c/o Self Help Nottingham, Ormiston House, 32-36 Pelham
Street, Nottingham NG1 2EG
Email info@depressionuk.org
www.depressionuk.org

A national mutual support group for people suffering from
depression.

Equilibrium – The Bipolar Foundation
John Eccles House, Robert Robinson Avenue, Oxford Science
Park, Oxford OX4 4GP
www.bipolar-foundation.org

Provides information about bipolar disorder, including the latest research, and an opportunity to share experiences.

Mood Gym*
https://moodgym.anu.edu.au/welcome

Mood Juice
www.moodjuice.scot.nhs.uk/depression.asp

NHS Choices
www.nhs.uk/Conditions/

NHS Direct
Helpline: 0845 46 47
www.nhsdirect.nhs.uk/

A 24-hour nurse-led helpline providing confidential healthcare advice and information.

Northumberland, Tyne and Wear NHS Foundation Trust
www.ntw.nhs.uk/pic/

Provides information and self-help leaflets on mental health.

MENTAL HEALTH
Action Mental Health (AMH) Northern Ireland
www.amh.org.uk/

Anxiety UK
Helpline: 08444 775 774
www.anxietyuk.org.uk; email and chat available through website

Promotes the relief and rehabilitation of persons suffering with anxiety disorders through information and provision of self-help services.

BEAT – Beating Eating Disorders
Helpline for adults (18+): 0845 634 1414
Email help@b-eat.co.uk
Helpline for young people (25 and under): 0845 634 7650
Email fyp@b-eat.co.uk
www.b-eat.co.uk

Provides helplines, online support and a network of nationwide self-help groups for adults and young people with eating disorders.

Breathing Space*
Tel: 0800 83 85 87
www.breathingspacescotland.co.uk

A free confidential service for people in Scotland experiencing low mood, depression or anxiety.

CALL – Mental health helpline for Wales
Helpline: 0800 132 737
http://callhelpline.org.uk/

Living Life to the Full*
www.llttf.com

Provides access to practical and user-friendly training in life skills, based on cognitive behaviour therapy.

Mental Health Ireland
www.mentalhealthireland.ie/

MIND
PO Box 277, Manchester M60 3XN
Infoline: 0300 123 3393
Email info@mind.org.uk
www.mind.org.uk

Provides advice and support to empower people experiencing a mental health problem. Campaigns to improve services, raise awareness and promote understanding.

No Panic
Unit 3 Prospect House, Halesfield 22, Telford TF7 4QX
Helpline: 0808 808 0545
www.nopanic.org.uk

Helps people who suffer from panic attacks, phobias, obsessive-compulsive disorders and other related anxiety disorders.

OCD–UK
Silverlands Lodge, Boarshead, Crowborough TN6 3HE
Tel: 0845 120 3778
Email support@ocduk.org
www.ocduk.org

Dedicated to improving the mental health and well-being of adults and children whose lives are affected by obsessive-compulsive disorder (OCD).

Rethink Mental Illness
Advice Team: 0300 5000 927
www.rethink.org

Provides advice and information, including free factsheets, for everyone affected by mental health problems.

Seasonal Affective Disorder Association (SADA)
PO Box 989, Steyning BN44 3HG
www.sada.org.uk

Informs the public and health professions about seasonal affective disorder, and supports and advises sufferers.

SANE
1st Floor, Cityside House, 40 Adler Street, London E1 1EE
Helpline: 0845 767 8000
www.sane.org.uk

Offers information and emotional support to anyone affected by mental illness, including family, friends and carers.

Scottish Association for Mental Health (SAMH)
Information service: 0800 917 3466 (Mon–Fri 2–4pm)
Email info@samh.org.uk
www.samh.org.uk

Provides information on community-based services, national campaigns and support for individuals.

Support in Mind Scotland
Tel: 0131 662 4359
Email info@supportinmindscotland.org.uk
www.supportinmindscotland.org.uk

Works to improve the well-being and quality of life of people affected by serious mental illness, including family members, carers and supporters.

Together – for mental well-being
www.together-uk.org

Provides services including advocacy, community support and skills and learning development for people with mental health issues.

Triumph over Phobias (TOPS)
PO Box 3760, Bath BA2 3WY
Email info@topuk.org
www.topuk.org

Helps sufferers of phobias, obsessive-compulsive disorder and other related anxiety to overcome their fears. Network of self-help therapy groups.

YOUNG PEOPLE
ChildLine (NSPCC)
Helpline: 0800 1111 (24 hours)
www.childline.org.uk; email and online chat accessible via website

Provides advice, support, topics and games for children and young people.

Family Lives
Helpline: 0808 8002222
http://familylives.org.uk; email and online chat accessible via website

Provides help and support for parents and carers in all aspects of family life.

The Lowdown
Helpline: 0808 802 4444 (Mon–Fri 10am–6pm)
www.getthelowdown.co.uk

A confidential guide to health for teenagers, including a comprehensive guide to the mind.

Papyrus
HopeLineUK: 0800 684141
www.papyrus-uk.org

Supports young people (35 years and under) at risk of suicide and those concerned about them.

Parents Helpline
Helpline: 0808 802 5544
Email parents@youngminds.org.uk
www.youngminds.org.uk and www.shareyourstory.org.uk
(parents' support forum)

Provide information and advice to parents with concerns about their child's emotional problems or behaviour.

TheSite.org
www.thesite.org/healthandwellbeing/mentalhealth

An online guide to life for 16–25 year-olds, providing non-judgemental support and information on everything from sex and exam stress to debt and drugs, including depression and self-harm.

Students Against Depression
www.studentdepression.org

Provides information, resources, discussion and real student stories.

Talk to Frank
Tel: 0800 776600 (free 24-hour line) or text 82111
www.talktofrank.com

Provides young people with information on drugs, including an A–Z.

Winston's Wish (childhood bereavement)
Helpline: 08452 03 04 05
www.winstonswish.org.uk

A charity for bereaved children, offering practical support and guidance to families, professionals and anyone concerned about a grieving child.

Youth 2 Youth
Helpline: 020 889 3675 (Mon–Fri 6.30–9.30pm)
www.youth2youth.co.uk; email and online chat accessible via website

Helpline service run by young people for young people aged 11–19 who feel they need confidential emotional support.

Youth Health Talk
www.youthhealthtalk.org and www.myyouthhelptalk.org
(support forum; requires registration)

Provides an A–Z of conditions and encourages talk about health and life in general.

Young Minds
Suite 11, Baden Place, Crosby Row, London, SE1 1YW
www.youngminds.org.uk

Charity committed to improving the emotional well-being and mental health of children and young people.

SUICIDE AND SELF-HARM
Befrienders Worldwide
www.befrienders.org/index.asp

Works worldwide to provide emotional support and reduce suicide.

Chooselife
www.chooselife.net

The national strategy and action plan on suicide prevention in Scotland.

National Self-Harm Network (NSHN)
PO Box 7264, Nottingham NG1 6WJ
Helpline: 0800 622 6000
www.nshn.co.uk

Offers support, advice and advocacy services to people affected by self-harm directly or in a care role.

The Samaritans
Tel: 08457 909090
Email jo@samaritans.org
www.samaritans.org.uk

A national organization of volunteers that seeks to alleviate emotional distress and reduce the incidence of suicide feelings and suicidal behaviour.

Survivors of Bereavement by Suicide
Helpline: 0844 561 6855
Email sobs.support@hotmail.com
www.uk-sobs.org.uk

Offers emotional and practical support to meet the needs and break the isolation of those bereaved by the suicide of a close relative or friend.

SAMH National Programme for Suicide Prevention
www.samh.org.uk/our-work/national-programmes/suicide-prevention

This link gives access to information, resources and support.

OTHER CONDITIONS AND SITUATIONS
ADD and ADHD
www.addandadhd.co.uk

Advice on attention deficit disorders and information on managing the conditions.

Age UK
Advice line: 0800 169 6565
www.ageconcern.org.uk

Works to improve later life for everyone by providing services and support. Website provides guidance on health and well-being, including depression.

Alcohol Concern
Helpline: 0800 917 8282 (freephone for landlines)
www.alcoholconcern.org.uk

Offers advice, information, factsheets and support on alcohol issues, plus a programme of training courses.

Alcoholics Anonymous
PO Box 1, 10 Toft Green, York YO1 7NJ
Helpline: 0845 769 7555
www.alcoholics-anonymous.org.uk

Offers advice and support on alcohol issues.

Alzheimer's Society
Helpline: 0300 222 11 22
www.alzheimers.org.uk

Works to improve the quality of life of people affected by dementia (sufferers and carers) in England, Wales and Northern Ireland.

Carers UK
Helpline: 0808 808 7777 (Wed–Thurs, 10am–12pm, 2pm–4pm)
www.carersuk.org and forum.carers.org (support forum)

Information, advocacy and network of local groups for carers of all kinds.

Carer Watch
www.carerwatch.com

A campaign group for carers that provides up-to-date information on the welfare reform programme.

Cinnamon Trust
Tel: 01736 757 900
www.cinnamon.org.uk

Seeks to relieve the anxieties and problems faced by elderly and terminally ill people and their pets.

Cruse Bereavement Care
Helpline: 0844 477 9400
Email helpline@cruse.org.uk
www.crusebereavementcare.org.uk

Provides free care to bereaved people and information, support and training services to those who are looking after them.

Drinkline
Tel: 0800 917 8282 (freephone for landlines)

Provides information and self-help materials, help to callers worried about their own drinking, support to the family and friends of people who are drinking and advice on where to go for help.

Electronic Medicines Compendium
www.medicines.org.uk/emc

Website has patient information leaflets (PILs) and data sheets on most prescribed drugs.

Miscarriage Association
Helpline: 01924 200799
Email info@miscarriageassociation.org.uk
www.miscarriageassociation.org.uk

Provides support and information regarding the distress associated with pregnancy loss.

Release
124–128 City Road, London EC1V 2NJ
Helpline: 0845 4500 215
Email ask@release.org.uk
www.release.org.uk

Offers advice and provide services for people using drugs and those who work with them.

Rape Crisis (England and Wales)
Helpline: 0808 802 9999
www.rapecrisis.org.uk

The national organization for rape crisis centres nationwide.

Royal British Legion
Helpline: 08457 725725
www.britishlegion.org.uk

Provides care and support to past and present members of the British armed forces and their families.

Stillbirth and Neonatal Death Society (SANDS)
Helpline: 020 7436 5881
Email helpline@uk-sands.org
www.uk-sands.org

A national charity providing support for bereaved parents

Survivors UK
Ground Floor, 34 Great James St, London WC1N 3HB
Helpline: 0845 122 1201
www.survivorsuk.org

Helps men who have been sexually abused and raises awareness of their needs.

Terrence Higgins Trust (HIV/AIDS)
www.tht.org.uk/myhiv

Online advice and free counselling (following registration) to help deal with HIV-positive diagnosis.

White.noise
www.whitenoise247.net

Provides free 24-hour audio of general background (or white) noise, or peaceful sounds to help sleep or with tinnitus or noise around you.

Women's Aid
Domestic violence helpline: 0808 2000 247
Email helpline@womensaid.org.uk
www.womensaid.org.uk

A national charity working to end domestic violence against women and children.

MONEY, LEGAL AND GENERAL HELP
Citizen's Advice Bureaux (CAB)
www.citizensadvice.org.uk

Local telephone directories and the CAB website give details of local offices. Provides free, independent and confidential advice on legal, money and other problems.

Community Legal Advice
Helpline: 0845 345 4345
Email help@communitylegaladviceorg.uk
www.communitylegaladvice.org.uk

A free confidential advice service paid for by legal aid that help with debt, housing, employment, education, benefit and tax credit problems.

Money Advice Service
Tel: 0300 500 5000
www.moneyadviceservice.org.uk

An independent government-funded service to help people manage their money better.

National Debt Line
Tel: 0808 808 4000
www.nationaldebtline.co.uk

Provides free confidential and independent advice on how to deal with debt problems.

Tax Credit Helpline
Helpline: 0345 300 3900
www.hmrc.gov.uk/taxcredits

Turn2us
www.turn2us.org.uk

A charitable service that helps people access the money available to them through welfare benefits, grants and other help.

PROFESSIONAL ORGANIZATIONS

British Association for Behavioural and Cognitive Psychotherapies (BABCP)
Imperial House, Hornby Street, Bury BL9 5BN
Tel: 0161 797 4484
Email babcp@babcp.com
www.babcp.com

Website includes directory of local practitioners.

British Association for Counselling and Psychotherapy (BACP)
BACP House, 15 St John's Business Park, Lutterworth LE17 4HB
Tel. 01455 883300
Email bacp@bacp.co.uk
www.bacp.co.uk

Website includes directory of local practitioners.

Counselling and Psychotherapy in Scotland (COSCA)
16 Melville Terrace, Stirling FK8 2NE
Tel: 01786 475 140
www.cosca.org.uk

The Royal College of Psychiatrists
17 Belgrave Square, London SW1X 8PG
Tel: 020 7235 2351 × 6259
Email reception@rcpsych.ac.uk
www.rcpsych.ac.uk

A catalogue of public education materials and leaflets is available from the Leaflets Department.

United Kingdom Council for Psychotherapy (UKCP)
2nd Floor, Edward House, 2 Wakley Street, London EC1V 7LT
Tel: 020 7014 9955
Email info@ukcp.org.uk
www.psychotherapy.org.uk

Website includes directory of local practitioners.

In the USA

Al-Anon/Alateen
Tel 1-888-425-2666
www.aa.org

Lists Al-Anon services in Canada, the USA and Puerto Rico. Local meeting information. Internet meetings.

American Association of Retired Persons
www.aarp.org

Security, protection and empowerment for older persons (50+). Information on depression, loss and grief.

American Foundation for Suicide Prevention
www.afsp.org

Has chapters nationwide. Offers information and support resources for those who have lost a loved one to suicide.

Anxiety Disorders Association of America
www.adaa.org

Debtors Anonymous
www.debtorsanonymous.org

Emotions Anonymous
www.emotionsanonymous.org
Local, online and telephone groups.

Freedom from Fear
www.freedomfromfear.org

Support groups for anxiety and depression. Online and email support.

National Alliance on Mental Illness
www.nami.org

A support and advocacy organization.

Obsessive Compulsive Foundation
www.ocfoundation.org

Families for Depression Awareness
http://familyaware.org

Information about depression and bipolar disorder.

Geriatric Mental Health Foundation
www.gmhfonline.org

Information on giving care, mental health topics relating to older adults and a depression recovery toolkit.

Mental Health America
www.nmha.org

Contact details for local support groups nationwide.

National Center for Post Traumatic Stress Disorder
www.ptsd.va.gov

National Suicide Prevention Lifeline
Tel: 1-800-273-TALK (1-800-273-8255) to connect to a national network of toll-free 24 hour crisis centers
www.suicidepreventionlifeline.org

National Women's Health Resource Center:
www.healthywomen.org

Downloadable publications on depression for women.

SAFE Alternatives
www.selfinjury.com

Information and resources for help with self-injury.

Self Inflicted Violence
http://healingselfinjury.org

Includes link to sample newsletter *The Cutting Edge*.

Yellow Ribbon
www.yellowribbon.org

Information and resources about suicide prevention for teens, parents and others. Some local contacts.

Index